Clawhammer Banjo
Tunes, Tips
& Jamming
by
Wayne Erbsen

Photo by Marte Clark

Sherman Hammons

©2015 Native Ground Books & Music, Inc.
Library of Congress Control Number 2015905297
Order Number NGB-203, ISBN 9781883206994
All arrangements ©2015 Fracas Music Co. (BMI)
Asheville, N.C. International Copyright Secured. All Rights Reserved.

Come visit us at www.nativeground.com

Contents

Contents

Instructional CD

Tucked into a sleeve on the inside front cover is an instructional CD loaded with 78 mp3 files that can be played on a computer. The recording is designed to augment the book and is not meant to be a stand-alone teaching guide. Every track is slow so you can play along with me after you get your feet wet. Throughout the book you'll find illustrations of an old gramophone with a number inside, which corresponds to a track on the CD. On each track, you'll hear a simple version of a tune played just like the tab. If I teach you any hot licks, they will be on the same track about 5 seconds later.

Thanks For Opening Me Up!

"Whew! Thanks for opening me up! I feel much better now. It's a rough life being a book sitting on a lonely shelf all day. As hard as I try, I can't teach anyone to play the banjo unless they open me up, turn the pages, and start reading what I've got to say. That's why I'm so excited to be in your hands right now. Trust me. These are the same hands that will soon be picking the banjo.

From my pages you're going to learn to play the 5-string banjo in clawhammer style. By the time you finish going through my pages, you'll know how to pick over forty tunes, you'll be prepared to join an old-time jam session, and you'll be exposed to the fascinating history of many of the tunes. Besides a banjo and me, you really don't need anything else except maybe a sense of humor, a bit of patience, and a dab of determination and spunk.

While I've got your attention, I'd like to introduce you to the author, Wayne Erbsen, who did all the plain and fancy writing. Wayne claims that he's been teaching banjo since dinosaurs roamed the earth, but I don't believe him one bit. I think it's more accurate to say he's been teaching banjo for about fifty years, which is only a drop in the bucket compared to the age of the tree I was sawed out of. I certainly will give him credit for one thing. He knows how to make difficult things both easy and fun. Some people have said that 'Wayne can even teach a frog to play the banjo.' He has certainly taught me a lot and I'm only a tree!

Fiddlin' Bill Hensley & Samantha Bumgarner

Now that I've said my piece, I'll keep quiet and turn it over to Wayne..."

Who This Book is For
1) Total beginners or novices on the banjo.
2) Intermediate players who want to learn new tunes and who dream of jamming with other musicians.
3) Advanced players who are "stuck" and need a little kick in the pants.
4) Grizzled old banjo players who think they know it all.
5) Bluegrass banjo players who want to dabble in clawhammer style.
6) People who think banjos are sexy and want to get a date. (Good luck!)
7) People who like their learning spiced with a pinch or two of humor.

The Banjo in Old-Time Music

Bascom Lamar Lunsford (fiddle)

Even though clawhammer banjo can be used to play quite a variety of music, it's a style that's most at home playing old-time music. In case you're new to this kind of music, let me tell you a little bit about it. Old-time music, as it's commonly defined, is music that is played for dances. Of course, we're not talking about the Twist or the Cha-Cha here. Instead, we're talking about clogging, flatfooting, square dancing and Virginia Reels. All of these dances require a strong one-TWO beat that works perfectly with the basic rhythm of clawhammer banjo: "claw-HAM-mer." Of course after a long night of dancing, many dance callers request that the band strike up a waltz. So, clawhammer banjo players have learned to accommodate waltz rhythms by changing their basic stroke from "claw-HAM-mer" to "claw-HAMmer-HAMmer."

Although playing up-tempo tunes at a dance is surely at the heart of old-time music, that's far from the whole picture. At practically any old-time jam around the country, in addition to countless fiddle tunes, you might also hear a few mournful ballads, songs from the minstrel stage, sentimental songs of lost love and tragedy, as well as an occasional gospel song or spiritual. All these types of songs (and more) can comfortably be played in the clawhammer style. In this book, I've included over forty tunes that cover most of the bases. You'll be introduced to a variety of tunes that fall loosely under the umbrella of old-time music.

The Book in a Nutshell

What you'll get in this book are old-time tunes that I've simplified down to their most basic level. I've stripped off all the variations and fancy licks to provide you only the bare-bones skeleton of each tune. I'll then show you a number of ways you can "dress" the skeleton by adding variations to each tune.

I use this approach because in Southern old-time music, musicians are given a fair amount of latitude to improvise on a tune without going completely hog wild. In contrast, many old-time players in the North and Midwest often attach more importance to the faithful re-creation of a distinct version that they have heard on a recording or perhaps from another old-time musician. Of course, there's nothing wrong with either approach. I just want to be clear that I'll be teaching you the naked skeleton of tunes. You can dress them any way you like, depending on whether they're going to dig a ditch, plow a field, or go to the ball. Sound good?

Other Names for Clawhammer
Beating, clobberhammer, downstroking, frailing, knocking, knockdown, rapping, thumb-cocking, thumping, whomping

Structure of Old-Time Music

In old-time music there are tunes and there are songs. Each has its own structure. First, let's talk about tunes.

Tunes: The most common type of tune in old-time music has two parts which are labeled A and B. Normally, the A part is played twice and then the B part is played twice. This is usually written out as AABB. You'll also run into tunes that have three parts (AABBCC), four parts (AABBCCDD), and even five parts (AABBCCDDEE).

The average tune will probably last between 2 1/2 and 3 minutes. However, if you're playing for a square dance, the tune might go on for 10 minutes or more. In some old-time jams, a tune can last so long that you can go out for lunch and come back and they're still playing that same tune!

Photo by Bob Lindsey

Rilla Ray

Songs vs. Tunes. Of course, the main difference between tunes and songs is that tunes are played instrumentally and songs are sung. Even though some tunes do have verses that are thrown in here and there, the words are mainly an afterthought. The main focus of a tune is on the playing, not the singing.

Songs, on the other hand, have the focus squarely on the vocals with the instrumentals taking a back seat. Some songs, like "Wild Bill Jones," are sung ballad style. On songs like this, you can expect a series of six or more verses all sung to the same melody. These kinds of songs are usually arranged with one or two verses separated by an instrumental rendition of the melody. In contrast to the ballad style, the majority of old-time songs are sung in verse-chorus style. This means the lead singer would sing the verses solo and one or more harmony singers would often join in on the chorus. Many times the verses and chorus are sung to the same melody, while on other songs, the verses and chorus each have their own melody.

What's the difference between a run over skunk and a run over banjo player? *The skunk was on his way to a gig.*

6

Tools & Equipment

Banjos have a lot of moving parts, so there's always something to tighten and adjust. I keep an old toolbox handy where I store everything I'll need to keep my banjo humming along like a Swiss watch: a bracket wrench, a small screw driver, extra strings and a wire cutter to clip off the ends when I install new strings.

A **capo** is a vital piece of equipment that you'll need practically every time you play with a fiddler. There are scores of excellent capos on the market, but the ones I prefer are capable of staying on the banjo at all times. That way, it'll be handy when you have a sudden banjo emergency. (See the image to the right with the capo firmly in place above the nut.)

To use the capo all you need to know is that if you're in G tuning and you want to get in the key of A, merely move your capo to the 2nd fret. If you're in double C tuning and you want to get in the key of D, capo up on the 2nd fret.

Photo by Wes Erbsen

Miniature railroad spike

Remember: For every fret you capo up, you'll need to raise the 5th string that same amount. Some people just crank up their 5th string from G to A and think nothing of it. I've broken too many strings that way, so I don't recommend that you try that. Instead, many music stores sell sliding 5th string capos that work pretty well. The solution I prefer is to have several miniature railroad spikes installed on the fingerboard of your banjo. When you're ready to raise the 5th string, merely slip the string under the lip of the railroad spike and you're good to go. I suggest having one spike installed at the 7th fret and another on the 9th fret. Many music stores have a repairman who can easily install the spikes for you.

Tip: If you use the railroad spike trick, keep in mind that the string has to take a slight detour to fit under the spike. This will make the string go slightly higher in pitch or sharper. After you slip the string under the spike, you'll normally have to tune the string down just a hair.

Tune List. One important piece of "equipment" is a tune list. Every time you learn a new tune, add it to the list. Even people who know hundreds of tunes often find it difficult to think of what to play when their turn comes to choose. Arrange your list in alphabetical order by tuning, just like the tunes in this book. With your trusty tune list, you'll never be at a loss when you can't think of a tune to play.

First Things First: Tuning

In this clawhammer banjo book we're going to learn to play in five tunings: double C, G, G modal, D modal and F. Don't fret! Each tuning will be clearly explained as we go along as well as on pages 109-111.

Why so many tunings? Because each tuning conveys a certain "atmosphere" in the words of the late, great banjoist Wade Ward from Independence, Virginia. If I were to only teach you tunes in G tuning, which is used almost exclusively in bluegrass banjo, you would be justified in thinking that you've been robbed by buying this book.

> The Notes in Double C Tuning:
> **1st = D, 2nd = C, 3rd = G, 4th = C, 5 = G**

We'll start out in what's called double C tuning. This means there are two Cs (the 2nd and 4th strings). The reason that we're starting with this tuning is because the melody can often be found on the 1st string. That will make the tunes in double C tuning much easier to play.

There are a number of different methods used to tune your banjo. First, start by memorizing the names of the notes of the strings in double C tuning (see the shaded box, above). Keep in mind that as you set the banjo on your lap, the 1st string is the string that's closest to the floor and the 5th string is closest to your chin.

Ed Young and Hobart Smith, 1959

1. Tuning the banjo to itself in double C tuning. 1) Tune the 1st string to a D note using an electronic tuner or any instrument that's already in tune (like a piano, a guitar, mandolin, fiddle or ukulele). 2) Fret the 2nd string at the 2nd fret and adjust that string until it sounds like the 1st string played open or unfretted. 3) Fret the 3rd string at the 5th fret and compare it to the 2nd string played open. Adjust as necessary. 4) Fret the 4th string at the 7th fret and make it sound like the 3rd string open. 5) Fret the 1st string at the 5th fret and tune the 5th string so it sounds like that note. That's it!

> Tuning Joke: Q) What does a banjo sound like when it's completely in tune? A) *No one knows.*

2. Tuning to an electronic tuner. Once considered a novelty, electronic tuners have become the gold standard for tuning most any instrument. Heck, I even have an app called "Clear Tune" on my cell phone. Most people prefer tuners that clamp onto the peghead of their instrument. The advantage of these tuners is that your hands are free to adjust the strings. Although I do think electronic tuners are a great and wonderful thing, make sure you can tune your banjo to itself, as in method 1 on the previous page.

3. Tuning to a guitar. The strings of the guitar are 1=E, 2=B, 3=G, 4=D, 5=A, 6=E. If you're trying to tune to a guitar player, there are several ways to do this. You can ask the guitar player

to play you a C chord. Once they play the C chord, your 2nd string should sound like their 2nd string, and your 4th string should sound like their 5th string. You can also just tune your 3rd or G string to the 3rd string on the guitar and go from there.

4. Tuning to a mandolin or fiddle. As you probably already know, a mandolin and a fiddle are tuned the same. The only exception is that many old-time fiddlers use what's commonly called "cross tuning," which means they tune their instrument so that some or all of the strings are tuned to the chord they're playing in (like A or D). However, if the fiddle is in standard tuning (sometimes called "Italian tuning"), the strings are 1=E, 2=A, 3=D, 4=G.

5. Tuning to a ukulele. The ukulele and also the banjo uke has become so popular that they're even showing up at old-time jams. Keep in mind that there are various sizes of ukuleles, all in different tunings. The most popular uke is the smallest size called the soprano. It's tuned 1=A, 2=E, 3=C, 4=G.

Lydia and William Williams

Tuning Tip #1. When you're tuning your banjo to itself (bottom of page 8), it's tempting to leave your left hand on the fretted note and reach over with your right hand to turn the peg. Please resist doing this! I've rarely ever seen a seasoned player tune this way. Instead, you should turn the peg with your left hand while you constantly play that note with your thumb. If you constantly play the note, you will be able to hear the string as it goes up or down. This little trick will help you get in tune much quicker. Scout's honor.

Tuning Tip #2. When you're comparing a tuned string to an untuned string, I suggest you play the tuned note first.

Tuning Joke: I just washed my ears and I can't do a thing with them.

How to Clawhammer

Clawhammering is a three step dance that you do with the fingers of your right hand. The rhythm of the clawhammer sounds like the word "claw-ham-mer." Once you get the hang of the basic stroke, you can play a billion tunes as easy as a frog jumping into a pond. Trust me. The clawhammer lick is really pretty easy. Let me show you.

Begin by curling up the fingers of your right hand, as in this 1856 painting by William Sidney Mount. Your fingers should be curved in a oval, as if you were gripping the handle of a broom or a baseball bat (if you don't sweep).

There are only three parts to the claw-ham-mer lick.

William Sidney Mount

The Banjo Player

1. With your hand in the claw shape, position your hand about an inch above the strings. Strike down on the 2nd string with your index or pointer finger. At the very same time, your thumb should come to rest on the 5th string (but don't sound it yet). We'll call this motion the "claw."

2. Lift up your "claw" and strike down on the 1st, 2nd and maybe 3rd strings with your middle and ring fingers. Again, your thumb should land silently on the 5th string. This is your "ham" of the claw-ham-mer.

3. Now that your thumb has come to rest on the 5th string, it's time to play the 5th string. This is the "mer" of the claw-ham-mer. That's all there is to it! **Remember:** The rhythm you want is "claw-ham-mer," "claw-ham-mer."

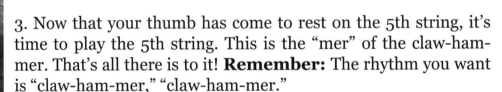

claw-ham-mer

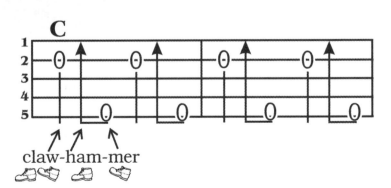

NOTE: The "claw" plays the melody on the 1st, 2nd, 3rd or 4th string. In the example above we're using the 2nd string as a melody note. Notice that it says "C." This means to continue to hold a C chord while you do the clawhammer.

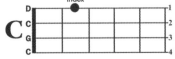

10

Clawhammer Tips

Tip#1. By far, the trickiest thing for beginners is making sure your thumb lands on the 5th string, as explained on page 10. Let me explain why this is so important. Bluegrass banjo players normally anchor their ring finger and/or pinky down on the head for stability and accuracy. Clawhammer players, on the other hand, are playing in the air. In order to hit the right string, you have to keep an eagle eye on your right hand to know what string to aim at. If your thumb constantly lands on the 5th string you have a frame of reference for hitting the melody string you want.

Tip #2. The second reason for constantly landing on the 5th string with your thumb is that sometimes after a melody note, you'll quickly want to hit the 5th string, which I call "thumbing." If your thumb is already on the 5th string, you can hit it instantly instead of having to hunt for it.

Photo courtesy of Jim Costa

Tip #3. It's a good idea to tap your foot when playing. When you play the "claw," your foot should go down and up. When you do the "ham," your foot should go down, and when you do the "mer," it comes up.

Tip #4. Be sure to give a good strong accent to the "ham," so it sounds like "claw-HAM-mer."

Tip #5. Remember that in the clawhammer style, you're always hitting down (toward the floor) and never up.

Tip #6. As you do the clawhammer lick, keep your hand fairly ridged, not floppy.

Tip #7. When I am clawhammering, I use my index or pointer finger to play the melody on the 2nd, 3rd, or 4th string. If the melody is on the 1st string, I use my middle finger. I much prefer using two different fingers to play the melody because it's less wear and tear on my fingernails. Having said that, I freely admit that some really great clawhammer players use only one finger to do all their melody picking, while others use two. You'll have to come up with the way that works best for you.

Learning The Clawhammer Lick

Words do a lousy job of properly explaining how to play the clawhammer lick.
To better help you learn, I've made several instructional videos that demonstrate
the clawhammer lick. They are all available on my website **www.nativeground.com.**

More Clawhammer Tips

Tip #8. You're going to need strong and fairly long fingernails on your right hand to play clawhammer style, especially if you want to be heard. Start growing your nails right now! I realize that some people cannot grow strong fingernails, or that they break them going about their every day life and work. Some people glue on artificial nails that they purchase at a drug store. Others actually get their picking nails "done" at a nail salon. In addition to these options, there are a wide array of plastic and metal finger picks that are used by clawhammers players. I could probably write an entire book on the various picks people have tried using – everything from cut up ping-pong balls to Dracula fangs. I would suggest checking the online forum Banjo Hangout, where people share all their success and horror stories using various kind of nail supplements and picks.

Photo by Wes Erbsen

Tip #9. As you're playing your clawhammer lick, you may have noticed that you can vary the tone of your banjo by moving your right hand closer to the bridge or further away. Many advanced clawhammer pickers generally keep their hand near where the neck meets the pot. However, you can decide for yourself where you get the best tone on your banjo.

Tip #10. Speaking of tone, many clawhammer banjo players like to dampen their banjo, to give a more muted tone. Some people stuff a rolled up rag or sock in the back between the dowel stick and the head. Again, you can decide if that's the kind of tone you want.

Tip #11. To get a good clean sound, you need to pay attention to how you're fretting the strings with your left hand. Of course, you want to avoid touching the metal frets with the fingers of your left hand. The easiest way to get a good sound is to firmly fret the string right behind the fret instead of directly between the frets.

Tip #12. To properly fret the strings, use only the very tips of your fingers. Make sure that the fingers of your left hand come almost straight down on the strings, not leaning over too much. Your thumb should be on the back of the neck, your left wrist slightly bent, and your fingers arched.

> **Almost Free Tuning Advice:**
> Tune the 1st string up until it breaks.
> Then tune the other strings to that.

Your Toolbox

Clawhammer banjo players use a variety of techniques to give their playing more pizazz. Here is a toolbox with some of the tricks of the trade. For each tune in this book, I will make suggestions about which tool to use. You can skip this page for now.

Pull-Off. Get in double C tuning (page 8) and fret the 1st string at the 2nd fret. Immediately after you hit that note with your right hand, use either the index or middle finger of your left hand to pull that fretted note down toward the floor so it makes a sound. The resulting sound means you're getting two notes, but you're hitting the strings with your right hand only once.

Clawhammer Pull-Off. This is a combination of the clawhammer lick and a pull-off. Just like we did above, fret the 1st string at the 2nd fret and pull that note off. This substitutes for the "claw" of the clawhammer. You'll then do the ham-mer of the clawhammer lick. So now instead of sounding like the word claw-ham-mer, it will sound like "claw-n-ham-mer."

Hammer-On. In double C tuning, play the 1st string open. Immediately after you play that note with your right hand, hammer down with the index or middle finger of your left hand on the 1st string, 2nd fret. Come down hard and fast on the string so it keeps ringing.

Clawhammer Hammer-On. Now we're going to combine the clawhammer with the hammer-on. Immediately after you do the hammer-on on the 1st string, 2nd fret, add the ham-mer. The rhythm of this also sounds like "claw-n-ham-mer."

Hammer-On & Pull-Off Combo. This combines the hammer-on and the pull-off with the ham-mer.

Slide. As the name suggests, a slide merely means that you slide up or down instead of playing the notes separately. For example, fret the 1st string at the 2nd fret. Hit that note and quickly slide up to the 1st string, 5th fret.

Clawhammer Slide. Just like we did with the pull-off and hammer-on, we can combine the slide with the clawhammer lick. Fret the 1st string, 2nd fret and slide up to the 5th fret. Then immediately add your ham-mer. The result will also sound like "claw-n-ham-mer."

Whacking is the term I use when I hit several strings at once. I do this when I want to give more punch to part of a tune.

Whack-Hammer. This combines the whack with the clawhammer. Instead of playing a single melody note as the "claw" of your "claw-ham-mer," now you'll whack all the strings followed by the "ham-mer." Be sure you're on a chord when you do this.

Your Toolbox

Bending Notes. To get a cool bluesy effect, especially on the tunes in G or D modal tuning, you can bend certain notes. Tune into G modal tuning (page 110) and fret the 3rd string, 3rd fret. Strike the string that you're fretting and either pull the string down, or push it up. If you're doing it right, it should sound like a stray calf calling for his mother.

 **Bent note with clawhammer lick**. You can easily combine a bent note with your clawhammer lick.

 **Thumbing**. When you have a series of several melody notes with no clawhammers, thumbing is a great way to fill in around those melody notes. All you do is quickly follow any melody note with a 5th or thumb string. On this track, I'm playing the 1st string open, 1st string 2nd fret, and 1st string 3rd fret with a 5th string between each.

Triple thumbing. Instead of playing a regular clawhammer lick, you can hit your 5th string three times quickly in a row. This is similar to what's called the Round Peak or Galax Lick. On this track you'll hear the first two measures of "Georgia Railroad" (page 54) using triple thumbing.

Photo by Carl Fleischhauer

Maggie Hammons

Drop-Thumb. When the melody is on the 1st string, you can drop your thumb down to the 2nd string and produce a rhythm like "claw-n-ham-mer." Here's how to practice this. First, get in double C tuning. Then lay the nail of your middle finger of your right hand on the 1st string and at exactly the same time, your thumb should come to rest on the 2nd string. Lift your hand up about an inch off the strings and practice landing on both strings at exactly the same time. Once you can do that, you should be able to play the 1st string with your middle finger quickly followed by the 2nd string played with your thumb. Then add the ham-mer. Taken together, it should all sound like "claw-n-ham-mer."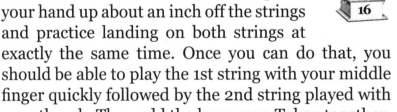

Banjo Jokes. Perhaps the most important tool in your toolbox is a good old banjo joke. For reasons too numerous to go into here, people love to poke fun at banjo players. Heck! Banjo players like to make fun of themselves. The truth is that banjo jokes serve an important function to keep you smiling when learning the banjo gets frustrating. As space allows, I'll throw in a banjo joke here and there throughout the book.

A Typical Page

Capo 2 to play in D

Where to capo to be in the key the tune is commonly played in

gCGCD - Key of C

The tuning. The lower case "g" is the 5th string. See pages 109-111 for a list of tunings

The key the tune is written out in

Track number on CD

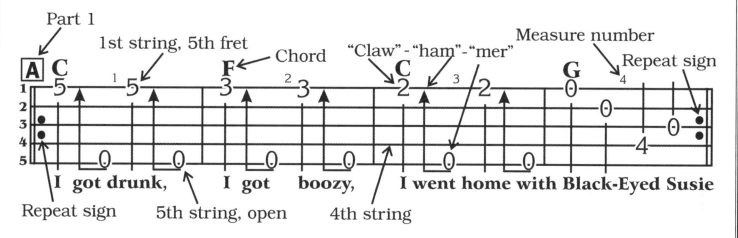

Part 1

1st string, 5th fret

Chord

"Claw"-"ham"-"mer"

Measure number

Repeat sign

I got drunk,   I got   boozy,   I went home with Black-Eyed Susie

Repeat sign

5th string, open

4th string

Note: This page shows the first line of "Black-Eyed Susie" (page 16) and contains many of the ingredients that you'll find throughout the book. All the important parts are diagramed for you. Take a few minutes to look over everything. Keep in mind that all the tunes are arranged in alphabetical order within five different tunings: double C tuning, G tuning, G modal tuning, D modal tuning and F tuning. You'll find several waltzes on pages 92-95. Instructions on all the tunings can be found on pages 109-111.

Another Note: Above each line of tab you'll notice the chords (eg. C, F and G). On pages 112-113, you'll find many of the basic chords. Sometimes, you won't actually need to go to the full chord because the melody may make playing the chord unnecessary. For example, there's a C chord at the very beginning of "Black-Eyed Susie," above. (A "C" chord is the 1st string, 2nd fret). However, the melody is the 1st string, 5th fret. Obviously, if you play the melody, you don't need to fret about the chord.

Final Note: In measure 4 above, there are four melody notes and it says to play a "G" chord. In a situation like this, you would ignore the "G" chord because you're not strumming or clawhammering the chord. It's merely there so other instruments will know what chord to play.

> If you're one of those people who like to eat your dessert first because you can't wait, then I invite you to play the tunes in this book in any order you want.

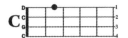 

Black-Eyed Susie

Some tunes are as old as dirt. "Black-Eyed Susie" certainly qualifies. It dates back to as early as 16th century England where it was known as "Three Jolly Sheepskins," and was used to accompany sword dances. It was also known as "Morris Off" when it was played for Morris dancing and processionals. In Ireland, it was commonly played as "Aillilliu mo Mhailin," which translates as "Alas My Little Bag." In America, it became a popular square dance tune throughout the 18th, 19th and 20th centuries. It was first recorded by Gid Tanner and Riley Puckett on March 8, 1924. Next to record it was Henry Whitter's Virginia Breakdowners on July 22, 1924.

"Black-Eyed Susie" is a great tune to start with. Many of the melody notes can be found on the 1st string, which makes it easy to play. We'll be playing it in double C tuning, which means it's in the key of C. This song has no set key that it's always played in. It all depends on finding a good key for your voice. In the box below, notice the keys some musicians have recorded it in.

> Ralph Stanley: **C**, Roscoe Holcolm: **B**, J.P. Nestor: **Bb**, Dan Gellert: **G**, Doc Roberts: **C#**, Fred Cockerham: **C#**, New Lost City Ramblers **C#**, Al Hopkins & His Buckle Busters: **G**.

Ice Cold Licks: Just go through and pick out only the melody notes. When you're comfortable with that, go back and add the clawhammer licks where indicated.

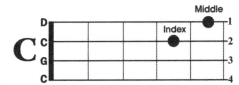

NOTE: In measure 1, it says to play a C chord while the melody is on the 1st string, 5th fret. In this case, you have two choices. You can ignore the C chord and just play that melody note. Or, you can also play a C chord that includes the 1st string, 5th fret (see illustration).

Warm Lick: If you use this C chord in measure 1, you can play a warm lick in measure 2. After you play this C chord, simply slide this chord down (in pitch) two frets so your index finger is on the 2nd string, 2nd fret and your middle finger is on the 1st string, 3rd fret. You are still playing the melody in measure 2, but now it has a cool harmony note to go with it. Try it!

Hot Lick: Slides (page 13) are one of the most fun variations on God's green earth. A good place to play a slide is the first note of the song. Fret the 1st string at the 2nd fret and slide up to the 1st string, 5th fret. It should sound like "claw-n-ham-mer."

Fingering: I suggest that you use your ring or pinky to play the 1st string, 5th fret, your middle finger to play the 1st string, 3rd fret, and your index finger to play the 1st string, 2nd fret.

NOTE: The chords are shown above the lines. Whenever there is a chord with no clawhammer stroke (eg. measure 14), you can ignore the chord. It's only there to guide your guitar player to the right chord.

Black-Eyed Susie

gCGCD - Key of C

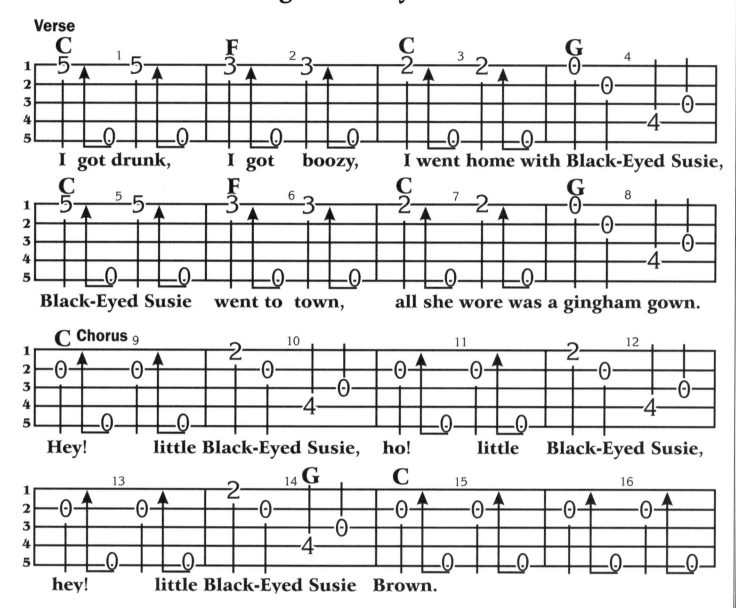

I got drunk, I got boozy, I went home with Black-Eyed Susie,

Black-Eyed Susie went to town, all she wore was a gingham gown.

Hey! little Black-Eyed Susie, ho! little Black-Eyed Susie,

hey! little Black-Eyed Susie Brown.

Hey old man I want your daughter,
To chop my wood and carry my water.

Black-Eyed Susie lives in a holler,
She won't come and I won't call her.

All I want in this creation,
Pretty little wife on a big plantation.

All I need to make me happy,
Two little boys to call me Pappy.

One name Sop and the other name Gravy,
One sop it up and the other gonna save it.

Black-Eyed Susie went huckleberry pickin',
Came home late and took a lickin'.

Love my wife and love my baby,
Love my biscuits sopped in gravy.

Black-Eyed Susie is long and lean,
Prettiest girl I ever seen.

Black-Eyed Susie's long and tall,
Sleeps in the kitchen, her feet in the hall.

Up Red Oak and down salt water,
Some old man gonna lose his daughter.

Cumberland Gap

E. M Hall

Let's take a little historical trip through the Cumberland Gap, which is where Kentucky, Virginia, and Tennessee come together. Sometimes referred to as the Gateway to the West, Native Americans traveled through the gap long before European and American travelers even knew it existed. In 1750, an explorer named Dr. Thomas Walker named the Cumberland River after Prince William, the Duke of Cumberland and the son of King George II of England. Eventually, the gap took on the name of the river.

The exact origins of the tune "Cumberland Gap" are elusive. There were several different melodies that were played throughout the 19th century using this title. The first commercial recording of "Cumberland Gap" was by Uncle AM Stuart, who recorded it in New York City in June of 1924. Although historically played in the key of G, we're going to learn a three-part version of "Cumberland Gap" using double C tuning. This three-part version started to make the rounds at southern fiddler's conventions in the mid to late 1970s. It is apparently a combination of two different versions. One was played by Tommy Jarrell, who learned it around 1915. The other was played by musicians like Norman Edmonds and Oscar Wright. No one seems to remember who merged these two versions into this three-part "festival version" in the key of D that is popular among old-time musicians today.

When you play this version of "Cumberland Gap" with other musicians, keep in mind that some people play the A part twice, as in this tab, while others play it four times. My best advice is to follow the fiddler to see how many times they play the A part.

Warm Licks: Pull-offs (page 13) are a good way to add some variations to "Cumberland Gap." In measure 3, you can pull off the 2nd fret on the 1st string and/or the 2nd fret on the 3rd string.

Hot lick #1: Sometimes, it's fun to strongly accent just one part of a tune. In the case of "Cumberland Gap," try whacking (page 13) a G chord at the very beginning of measure 5. Instead of playing the regular "claw-ham-mer" lick there, play "whack-ham-mer."

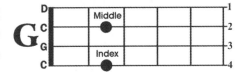

Hot lick #2: You can add some punch to the beginning of the C part by playing a hammer-on to the first note of measure 9. If you like, you can also add a hammer-on (page 13) to the first note of measure 11.

Note: In measure 2 you can ignore the F chord and just fret the 1st string at the 7th fret. You can also ignore any chord that does not have a clawhammer with it (eg. measure 3 and 7).

Capo 2 to
play in D

Cumberland Gap

gCGCD - Key of C

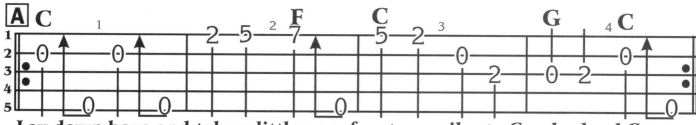

Lay down boys and take a little nap, fourteen miles to Cumberland Gap.

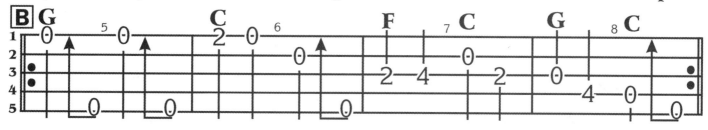

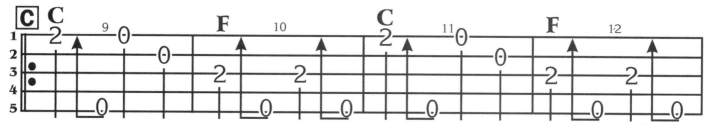

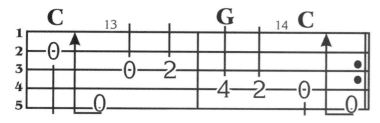

Lay down boys and take a little nap,
14 miles to Cumberland Gap.

Lay down boys and take a little nap,
Snow knee-deep in Cumberland Gap.

Cumberland Gap's a devil of a place,
Couldn't find water to wash my face.

Me and my wife's pap,
Walked all the way from Cumberland Gap.

Pretty little girl if you don't care,
I'll leave my demijohn a-sittin' right there.

If it ain't there when I get back,
I'll raise hell in Cumberland Gap.

Lay down boys and take a little rest,
We'll all wake up in a whippoorwill's nest.

I'm going back to Cumberland Gap,
To see my granny and my grandpap.

Me and my wife and my little chap,
Made a good living on Cumberland Gap.

Saved my money and bought me a farm,
Raise sweet taters as long as your arm.

Someone once heard Tommy Jarrell singing this last verse and thought the lyrics were "long as yarn."

East Virginia

In the mid-1920s, many old-time musicians from the southern mountains flocked to portable studios in places like Asheville, North Carolina and Bristol, Virginia to audition to make records. Those who managed to impress talent scouts like Ralph Peer, Frank Walker or Eli Oberstein often received a flat rate of $25 per song, which was nothing to sneeze at in those days.

Among the first songs recorded in those early days was "East Virginia." The roster of names that recorded it reads like a Who's Who of early country music: Buell Kazee (4/20/27), B.F. Shelton (9/29/27), Clarence Ashley (10/23/1929), Ashley & Foster (09/06/1933), The Carter Family (05/08/34 and 05/07/1935), Karl & Hardy (10/07/1936) and Roy Acuff (10/22/36).

In my book *Clawhammer Banjo for the Complete Ignoramus*, I included a spooky version of "East Virginia" in G modal tuning that was loosely based on the recordings of Clarence Ashley and B.F. Shelton. In contrast to that, this is a more upbeat version of "East Virginia" that is more or less based on the two recordings of the song by the Carter Family.

Warm Lick: Throw in a hammer-on (page 13) at the beginning of measures 1, 2 or 3 on the 1st string, 2nd fret.

Hot lick #1: You can play a pull-off (page 13) on the 1st string, 2nd fret on any or all of these measures: 2, 3, 11, 12 and 14.

Hot lick #2: At the end of measures 4 and the beginning of measure 5 you can slide from the 1st string, 5th fret to the 1st string 7th fret. You'll have to hurry to get to the F chord pictured here. If you'd like to skimp on the F, you can simply fret the 1st string, 7th fret and the 2nd string, 5th fret and only play those notes on your "ham-mer." If you like the results of this slide, you can also do it in measures 8-9.

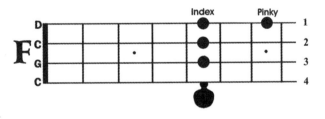

NOTE: Playing "East Virginia" requires you to be somewhat "athletic" because the melody

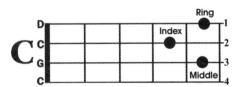

leaps from the 2nd to the 5th fret. If you'd like to take a lazier approach, simply hold down this C chord for the "claw" and the "hammer." It contains all the notes you need to play measures 1, 2, 3, and 4 as well as 7, 8, 11 and 12. Here's how it works: 1st string, 2nd fret=2nd string, 4th fret; 2nd string open = 3rd string, 5th fret.

How many banjo players does it take to screw in a light bulb?
Five. One to screw it in and four to lament about how much they miss the old one.

East Virginia

gCGCD - Key of C

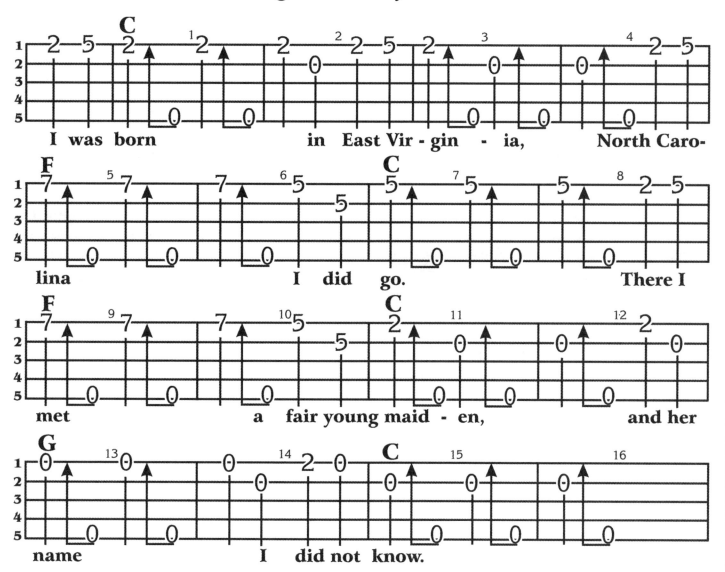

I was born in East Virginia,
North Carolina I did go,
There I met a fair young maiden,
And her name I did not know.

Oh her hair was dark and curly,
And her lips were ruby red,
On her breast she wore white lilies,
Where I longed to lay my head.

I don't want your greenback dollar,
I don't want your watch and chain,
All I want is your heart darling,
Say you'll take me back again.

The ocean's deep and I can't wade it,
And I have no wings to fly,
I'll just get me a blue-eyed boatman,
For to row me over the tide.

I'll go back to East Virginia,
North Carolina ain't my home,
I'll go back to East Virginia,
Leave those North Carolinians alone.

Tip: Instead of playing the 1st string, 5th fret in "East Virginia," you can simply play the 5th string open with your thumb.

21

C

Fall on My Knees

Am

Photo by Bosco Takaki

Tommy Jarrell

Every summer in the early 1970s, I used to jump in my 1964 Volvo sedan and travel to a different fiddlers convention in the South. In the back seat, I stacked my fiddle, banjo, mandolin and guitar. On top of that I threw my sleeping bag and a paper bag that held my provisions, which usually consisted of a jar of peanut butter and a loaf of bread. Back then, it seemed like almost every community in southwest Virginia and western North Carolina held their own little fiddlers convention that was put on to raise money for the Lions Club or the local fire department. Besides the fun of competing for ribbons and cash prizes, it was great to meet some of the old-timers who came out of the hills with their banjos and fiddles to compete and jam.

One of the greatest musicians of the older generation that I got to know at these conventions was Tommy Jarrell. Although he never entered any of the contests, he was there to play music with about anybody who would join in...and a lot of us did. It was from Tommy that I learned this version of "Fall on My Knees," who said he first heard the tune in about 1915.

"Fall on My Knees" is a Surry and Grayson County, Virginia version of an older folk song known as "Lonesome Road" or "Look Up and Down That Lonesome Road." It appeared in Carl Sandburg's book, *The American Songbag* (1927) and has been recorded by everyone from Joan Baez, Doc Watson and even that scoundrel, Wayne Erbsen.

Playing "Fall on My Knees" is about as easy as eating apple pie. If you make your C chord with your middle finger you can easily play the A minor (Am) chord by adding your index finger to the 3rd string, 2nd fret.

Hot Licks #1: When the melody goes up to the 1st string, 2nd fret in measures 3, 5, and 9, you can play a hammer-on. The second time there is a 1st string, 2nd fret in those same measures, you can play a pull-off.

Hot Lick #2: You can play a hammer-on-pull-off combo in measures 3, 5 and 9.

Fall on My Knees

gCGCD - Key of C

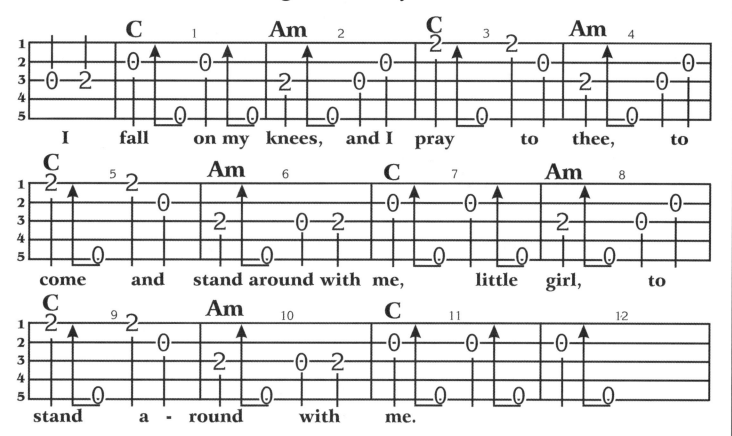

I fall on my knees, and I pray to thee, to

come and stand around with me, little girl, to

stand a - round with me.

Look up, look down, that lonesome old road,
Hang down your little head and cry, little girl,
Hang down your little head and cry.

There's more than one, Lord, there's more than two,
No other woman like you, little girl,
No other woman like you.

I wish to the Lord that I'd never been born,
Or died when I was young, little girl,
Or died when I was young.

I never would have kissed your red, rosy cheeks,
Or heard your lying tongue,
Or heard your lying tongue.

You've told me more lies than there's stars in the skies,
You'll never get to heaven when you die, little girl,
You'll never get to heaven when you die.

My suitcase is packed and my trunk is unsewn,
Goodbye little woman, I'm gone, I'm gone,
Good-bye little woman, I'm gone.

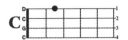 C

Hang Me

 F

Some newfangled songs are written by fancy-pants songwriters who sit in their air conditioned offices writing about hard times. This song, on the other hand, is the real deal. It could not be any more real if it tried. The outlaw captured in this song was reportedly hung for murder in Fort Smith, Arkansas in the 1870s. If so, chances are good that he was sentenced to die by the famous hanging judge himself, the Honorable Isaac Charles Parker. From 1875 to 1896 Judge Parker had jurisdiction over Oklahoma and all of the Indian Territories. Over those 21 years, he tried over 13,500 cases and sentenced 160 men to death. Of that number, 79 were hanged during his term of office. During the first fourteen years he was on the bench, the convicted could seek no appeal, save from heaven.

Parker's chief executioner was George Maledon, who took great pride in his "scientific" hangings. Of the 79 men sentenced to death by the Hanging Judge, Maledon personally hanged 60. When he finally retired, he went on the lecture circuit where he proudly displayed several of his favorite hanging ropes.

"Hang Me" is also known as "I've Been All Around This World" and is nearly perfect the way it is. However, it wouldn't hurt to add a few hot licks just for spice.

Finger Placement: You'll need to use your ring finger or pinky to play the 4th string, 4th fret. You're really supposed to keep your index finger on the 1st string, 2nd fret (a C chord) at the same time. For some of you with small hands, this might seem next to impossible. If you find yourself in that pickle you can forget about holding down the C chord.

Hot lick #1: You can add a hammer-on to the 4th string, 4th fret in measures 1 and 12.

Hot lick #2: Use a pull-off occasionally on any of the 4s in this song. But remember that just like hot sauce, a little goes a long way!

If you still want to pour on the heat, try a pull-off on the 2 in measure 6.

Hot lick #3: To add some pizazz, you can use the whack-hammer lick at the beginning of measure 5 where it goes to a G chord. To give you more strings to whack, I suggest you play this G chord.

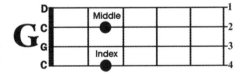 G

Hot lick #4: You can do a slide (page 13) from the 2 to the 4 in measure 13, 3rd beat.

A man hears from his doctor that he only has six months to live. He begs the doctor for help. Finally, the doctor advises him to move to Cleveland and marry a woman who's learning to play banjo. He asks the doc if that will make him live longer. Doc says, *"No, but it will seem longer."*

Hang Me

gCGCD - Key of C

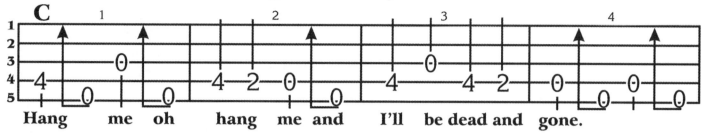

Hang   me   oh   hang   me   and   I'll   be dead and   gone.

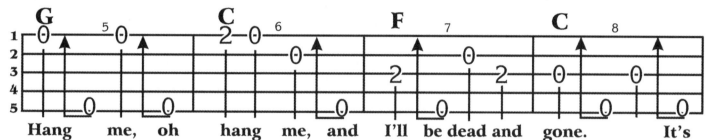

Hang   me,   oh   hang   me,   and   I'll   be dead and   gone.   It's

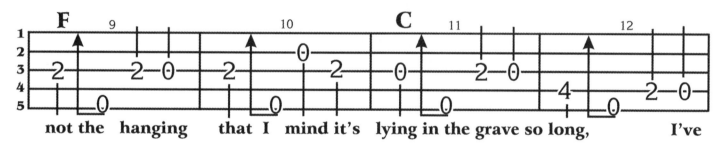

not the   hanging   that I   mind it's   lying in the grave so long,   I've

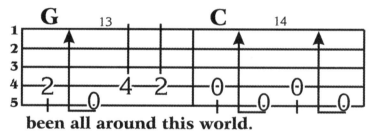

been all around this world.

Working on the new railroad with mud up to my knees, (2X)
Working for big John Henry and he's so hard to please,
I've been all around this world.

Up on the Blue Ridge Mountains, it's there I'll take my stand, (2X)
With a rifle on my shoulder, six shooter in my hand,
I've been all around this world.

Lulu, oh Lulu come and open up the door, (2X)
Before I have to open it with my old .44,
I've been all around this world.

When you go a fishing, take a hook and line, (2X)
When you go a courting don't never look behind,
I've been all around this world.

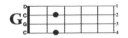

C

Mole in the Ground

G

Jim Bollman Collection

Bascom Lamar Lunsford, who famously called himself "the Squire of South Turkey Creek," was the first to record "I Wish I Was A Mole in The Ground" on March 15, 1924. This recording marked the first time that anyone had recorded on the 5-string banjo in what would later be called country music. For that, we tip our hat to Mr. Lunsford. He later recalled that he learned the song from Fred Moody in 1901 when they were both students at Rutherford College. Lunsford insisted that the use of the word "bend" referred to a bend in the Pigeon River that runs through Haywood County.

In 1952, Lunsford's version of "I Wish I Was Mole In The Ground" was reissued in Harry Smith's influential record set, "Anthology of American Folk Music." It was from this record that the song became widely known among fans of old-time music. In the notes to this set of records, Smith disputes Lunsford's claim about the meaning of the word "bend." Smith suggests that the word was actually "pen," and that it referred to Big Bend Penitentiary. Against my better judgement, I'm taking sides and sticking with Lunsford on this.

Hot Lick #1. A great way to decorate "Mole in the Ground" is to use slides. Any time you see the 4th string at the 4th fret, you can slide into it. Simply fret the 4th string, 2nd fret, and slide up to the 4th fret.

Hot Lick #2. At the beginning of measures 5 and 9, the melody goes up to the 1st string, 2nd fret followed by a "ham-mer." This would be a perfect place to add a hammer-on. All you do is play the 1st string open, then quickly hammer down on the 1st string, 2nd fret.

Fudging the Chords. In measures 2 and 14, "Mole in the Ground" goes quickly to a G chord and then back to the C. It's certainly difficult to get to the G chord fast enough. When I play it, I often fudge and skip the G chord entirely. All I do is play the open strings on the "ham-mer." Feel free to do this same thing. But for goodness sake, don't tell anybody you're doing this. Let's just make it our little secret. OK?

What will you never say to a banjo player? *"That's a nice Porsche."*

Mole in the Ground

gCGCD - Key of C

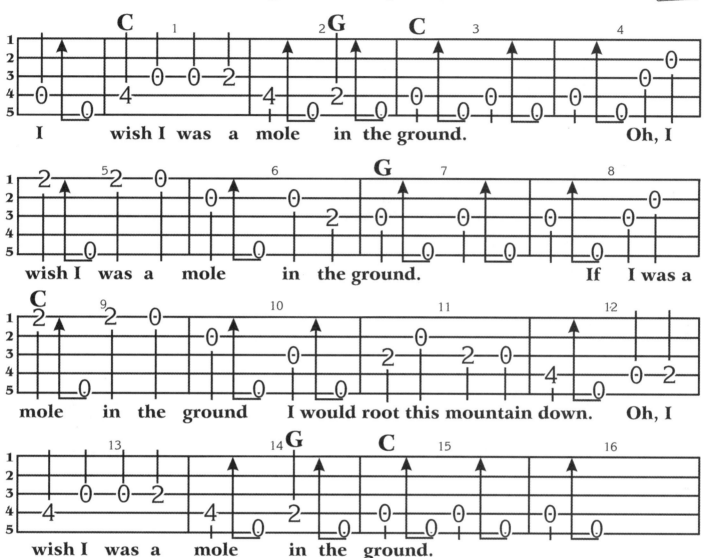

I wish I was a mole in the ground. Oh, I wish I was a mole in the ground. If I was a mole in the ground I would root this mountain down. Oh, I wish I was a mole in the ground.

I've been in the bend so long,
I've been in the bend so long,
I've been in the bend with the rough
   and rowdy men,
It's baby where you been so long?

I don't like a railroad man,
No, I don't like a railroad man,
A railroad man will kill you when he can,
And drink up your blood like wine.

I wish I was a lizard in the spring,
I wish I was a lizard in the spring,
If I was a lizard in the spring,
I could hear my darlin' sing,
I wish I was a lizard in the spring.

Photo by Michael Keller

Lester McCumbers

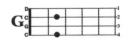

F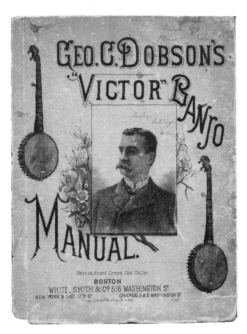

Needlecase

G

It was Sam McGee, the legendary musician from the Grand Ole Opry, who helped popularize "Needlecase" with his 1957 recording for Folkways Records. Even though the tune was reportedly popular in Alabama in 1929, I can find no record that it was ever commercially recorded during what was called "the golden era of country music."

I remember teaching "Needlecase" to my banjo and fiddle classes at the Augusta Heritage Workshop in Elkins, West Virginia in the mid seventies. In recent years, it has become quite popular at some jams. No wonder! It is an infectious little tune that's sure to get stuck in your head.

Hot Lick #1. Right from the get-go, you can accent the first beat of the song. Instead of playing the 1st string, 5th fret in measure 1, you can just kind of whack the 1st, 2nd and 3rd strings while you hold down the 1st string at the 5th fret.

Hot Lick #2. Adding a few pull-offs can add spice to this tune. In measures 1, 3 and 5, you can a pull-off on the 1st string, 5th fret, the 1st string 3rd fret and/or the 1st string, 2nd fret.

Hot Lick #3. If you'd like to get really fancy, you can combine the whack from hot lick #1 with a pull-off on the 1st string, 5th fret. I guess we should give it the name "whack-pull."

Marcus Martin

"Music is for the upbuilding of man. It is the most high thing." Legendary fiddler Marcus Martin

Needlecase

gCGCD ~ Key of C

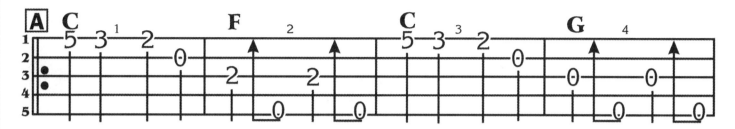

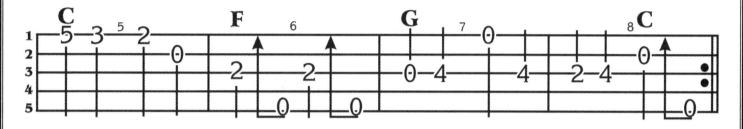

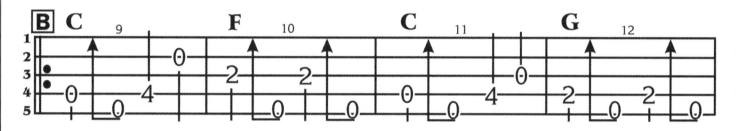

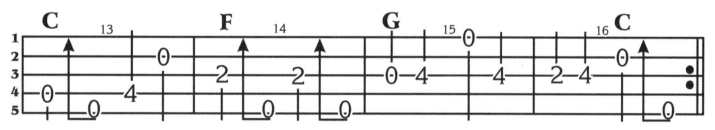

Manly Reece

Courtesy of Andy Cahan

Oh My Little Darling

One of the things that makes "Oh My Little Darling" interesting to play is that most of the melody notes can be found on the 1st string. In measure 3, for example, there are four of these melody notes in a row, which makes fingering with your left hand a little tricky.

Fingering: Maybe this is as good a time as any to talk about which finger to use when. The general rule for the average song is to use a different finger whenever you play on a different fret. If you skip a fret, you should skip a finger. However, "Oh My Little Darling" might be an exception to this rule. In measure 3 you can certainly use a different finger for each fret. But in this case, I would use my index finger to play the 5 and my ring finger to play the 7, 8 and the 7 again. Then I would use my index finger to fret the 3 in measure 4. You can experiment to see what works best for you. The main thing to keep in mind is that you'll want to move your hand as short a distance as possible to get the job done. There's not one right way to finger these notes.

Note: In measure 2, in order to get the melody to come out right, we're doing a rhythm that sounds like "claw-claw-hammer-hammer."

Hot Lick #1. In measure 1, you can add a hammer-on to the 1st string, 2nd fret. You can do the same thing in measures 7 and 15, when the melody is on the 1st string, 2nd fret.

Hot Lick #2. Whenever there are two or more individual notes without a claw-hammer (eg. measures 2, 3, 6, 7, 10, 14 and 15, you can add thumbing, which means you can play the 5th string quickly after some or all of those notes.

Hot Lick #3. On the first note in measure 9, you can do a whack-hammer.

Hot Lick #4. In measure 9 when you're on the 10th fret, after you hit that note, you can quickly slide **down** that string to about the 7th fret. To me, this is like taking a quick roller coaster ride, and is quite fun. For added zip, you can combine the slide with the whack-hammer.

What's the difference between an onion and a banjo? *Nobody cries if you cut up a banjo.*

Oh My Little Darling

gCGCD - Key of C

They don't write 'em like this one anymore and maybe they never did. It was recorded in 1939 for the Library of Congress by Thaddeus C. Willingham, an Alabama banjo player. It's kind of a rare tune, and you almost never hear it, but it has a strong melody that's really fun to play.

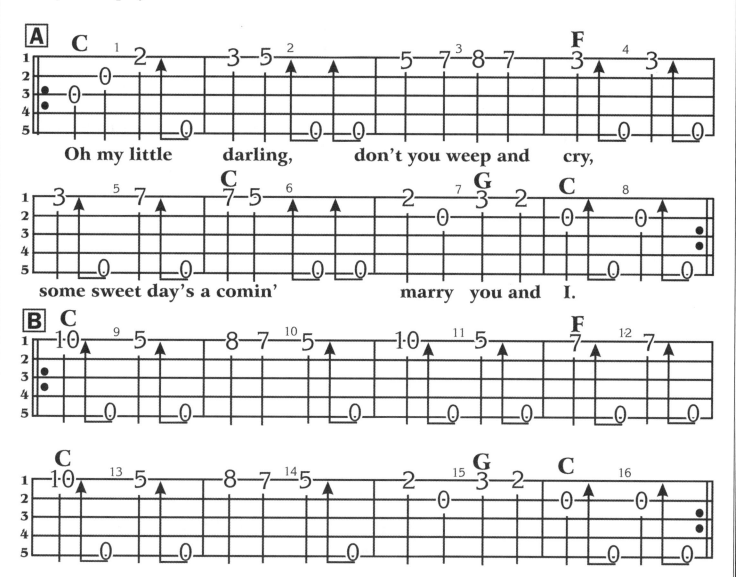

Oh my little darling,
Don't you weep and cry,
Some sweet day's a comin'
Marry you and I.

Up and down the river,
Cross the county line,
Pretty little girl's a-laughing
My wife is always cryin'.

Jimmy drive the wagon,
Jimmy hold the line,
Bust my sides a-laughing
To see those horses flyin.'

Oh my little darling,
Don't you weep and moan,
Some sweet day's a-comin'
Carry my darling home.

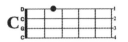

Old Plank Road

Uncle Dave Macon

No self-respecting banjo book would even dream of not including at least one tune by Uncle Dave Macon. Uncle Dave was irrepressible. He was the first star of the Grand Ole Opry, where on Saturday nights he would flog the living daylights out of the banjo while he hooted and hollered and stamped his feet. Starting with his very first Opry performance in December of 1925, Uncle Dave brought his banjo styles and old-time songs into the living room of countless rural Southerners via the miracle of radio. He single-handedly kept the 5-string banjo alive at a time when the tenor banjo was king. It wasn't until Earl Scruggs joined Bill Monroe's Blue Grass Boys on the Opry in late 1945 that the banjo had a new champion. After witnessing Earl's performance, Uncle Dave quipped, "That boy can play banjo, but he ain't one bit funny."

By all means, you should do yourself a big favor and listen to Uncle Dave do what he called "Way Down the Old Plank Road." His uproarious performance captures him in his prime, beating out rhythms with his feet while he shouted and carried on like a man possessed.

Chords. The only chords you need to play on "Old Plank Road" are C and G. You can ignore the F because there's no "hammer" on that chord.

Hot Lick. To try to achieve some of the explosive zest that Uncle Dave gets on "Old Plank Road," we need to add some "whacks." On the chorus, any time you see the word "won't," whack a C chord. (This also happens to be the melody note.) So what you end up with is, "**Whack** get drunk no more, **Whack** won't get drunk no more," and so on.

String Band N.C. State Prison.

Courtesy of Mike Cooke

Old Plank Road

gCGCD - Key of C

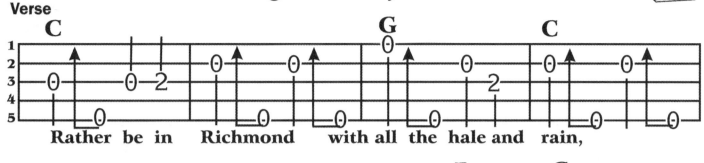

Rather be in Richmond with all the hale and rain,

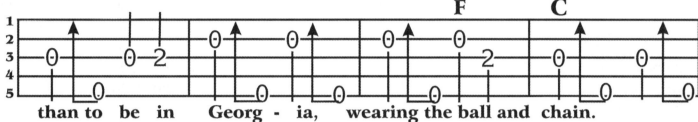

than to be in Georg - ia, wearing the ball and chain.

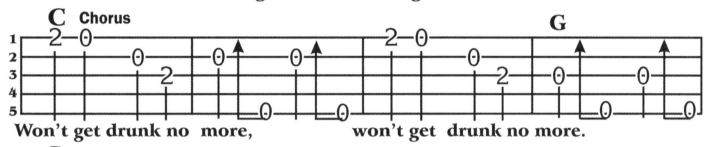

Won't get drunk no more, won't get drunk no more.

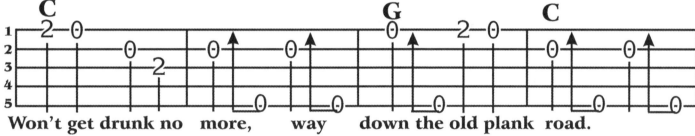

Won't get drunk no more, way down the old plank road.

I went down to Mobile, but I got on the gravel train,
Very next thing they heard of me, had on that ball and chain.

Doney, oh dear Doney, what makes you treat me so,
Caused me to wear that ball and chain, now my ankle's sore.

Knoxville is a pretty place, Memphis is a beauty,
Wanna see them pretty girls, hop to Chattanoogie.

I'm going to build me a scaffold on some mountain high,
So I can see my Doney girl as she goes riding by.

My wife died on Friday night, Saturday she was buried,
Sunday was my courtin' day, Monday I got married.

Eighteen pounds of meat a week, whiskey here to sell,
How can a young man stay at home, pretty girls look so well.

Rabbit in a Log

Monroe Brothers

Also known as "Have a Feast Here Tonight," this song has been embraced by both old-time and bluegrass musicians. It makes a dandy solo banjo piece, or is also great played with a band.

Bill and Charlie, the Monroe Brothers, did such a powerful performance on their January 28, 1938 recording of this song that I was convinced they had written it. Come to find out, it's a much older song that was cobbled together out of bits and pieces of older songs by the Prairie Ramblers. The Monroe Brothers got to see the Prairie Ramblers in action when they were all performers on the National Barn Dance in Chicago, starting in 1932. Interestingly enough, the Monroe Brothers were part of a dance team, not a musical ensemble. By the way, you might remember the Prairie Ramblers because they were the band that backed up Patsy Montana on the first million seller for a female performer in country music with her 1936 recording of "I Want to be a Cowboy's Sweetheart."

There's really not that many hot licks that are appropriate to play on "Rabbit in a Log." Instead, you should concentrate on just playing a good, solid version at a pretty good clip...like a spooked rabbit.

NOTE: "Rabbit in the Log" is too long to fit on one page. When you finish playing the bottom line of tab, go back up and play the third and fourth lines. The song finally ends when you play the 1st half of measure 16.

I'll build me a fire and I'll cook that old hare,
I'll roll him in the flames and bake him brown.
Have a feast here tonight while the moon is shining bright,
Then find myself a place to lie down.

To lie down (to lie down), to lie down (to lie down),
Then find myself a place to lie down.
Have a feast here tonight while the moon is shining bright,
Then find myself a place to lie down.

There's a chicken on my back, the bloodhounds on my track
The soles of my shoes are nearly gone;
Just a little ways ahead there's a barn or a shed,
That's where I'll rest my weary bones.

Weary bones (weary bones,) weary bones (you lazy bones),
That's where I'll rest my weary bones,
Just a little ways ahead there's a barn or a shed,
That's where I'll rest my weary bones.

Rabbit in a Log

gCGCD - Key of C

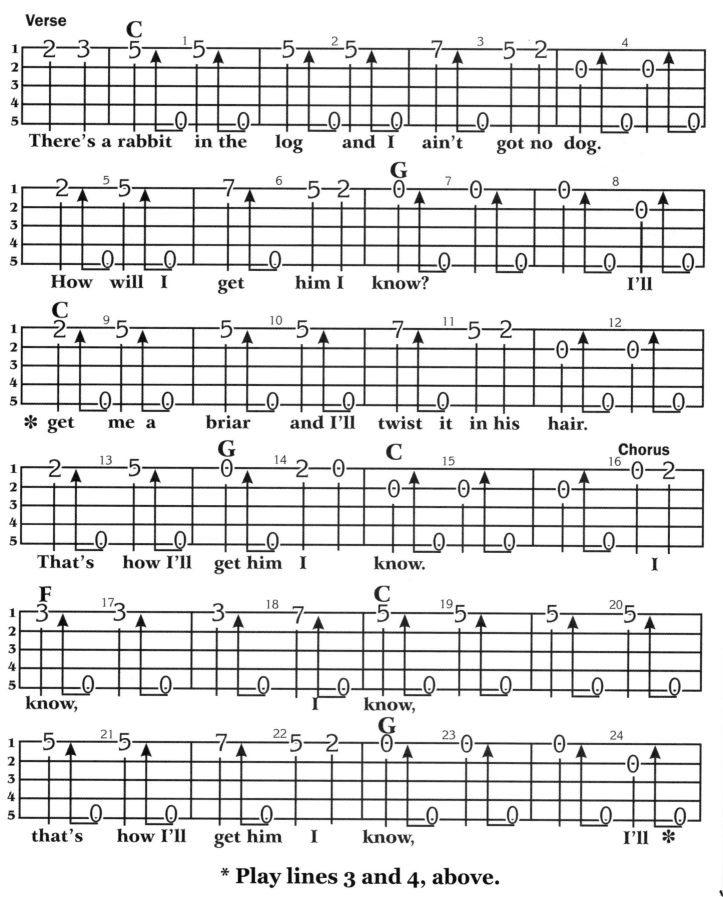

Verse

There's a rabbit in the log and I ain't got no dog.

How will I get him I know? I'll

* get me a briar and I'll twist it in his hair.

That's how I'll get him I know. **Chorus** I

know, I know,

that's how I'll get him I know, I'll *

* Play lines 3 and 4, above.

Rock That Cradle Lucy

gCGCD - Key of C

28

It's high time we learn a tune from the repertoire of Gid Tanner and His Skillet Lickers. "Rock That Cradle Lucy" started out in 1843 as "Miss Lucy Long," as performed by the Virginia Minstrels. It was soon picked up by other minstrel troops and before the end the decade, it was the most popular tune on the minstrel stage.

Gid Tanner

Hot Lick #1. You can add a hammer-on to the 2nd fret at the very beginning of measure 1. In fact, you can do the same thing any time you have the 1st string, 2nd fret followed by a "ham-mer."

Hot Lick #2. This tune is a good one to add some thumbing. After any of the single melody notes on the 1st string, such as in measures 3 and 7, simply play the 5th string quickly with your thumb. **Note:** There are no lyrics to the B part.

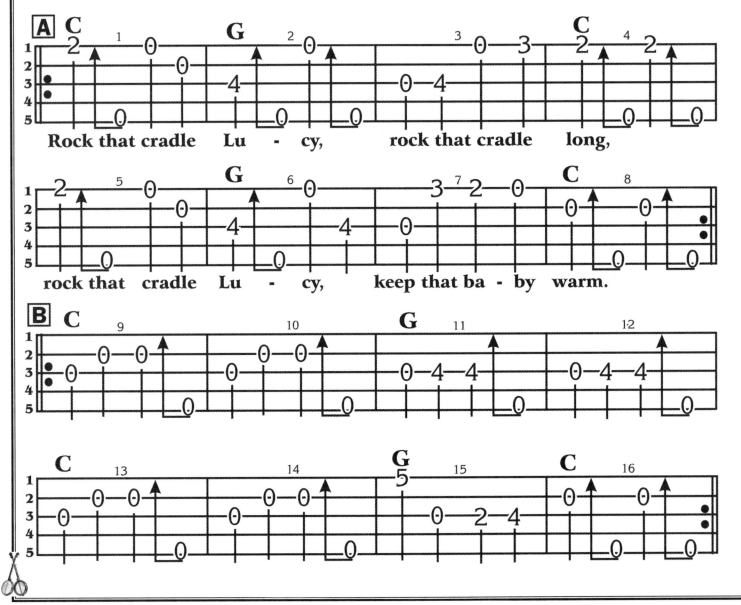

Capo 2 to
play in D

Rock That Cradle Joe

gCGCD - Key of C

Not to be confused with "Rock That Cradle Lucy," this tune is a current favorite at festivals and old-time jams. This version is one that has evolved from a 1940s home recording of J.W. Spangler and his second cousin Dudley Spangler, both of Meadows of Dan, Virginia. J.W.'s given name was John Watts Spangler, but he went by the name of "Babe Spangler." Born on November 15, 1882 in Patrick County, Virginia, his father was a respected fiddle player in the area. Until losing his sight in 1920 due to congenital glaucoma, Babe worked as a guard at the state penitentiary in Richmond, Virginia. As his sight declined, Babe became more involved in music, frequently performing as "The Old Virginia Fiddler" on the *Corn Cob Pipe Show* on Richmond's radio, WRVA. In 1927, Babe won the Virginia State Fiddlers contest. He died at the ripe old age of 92.

Hot Lick. "Rock That Cradle Joe" offers many opportunities to use hammer-ons. Any time the melody is on the 1st string, 2nd fret followed by a ham-mer, you can play the 1st string open, and then hammer on to the 1st string, 2nd fret.

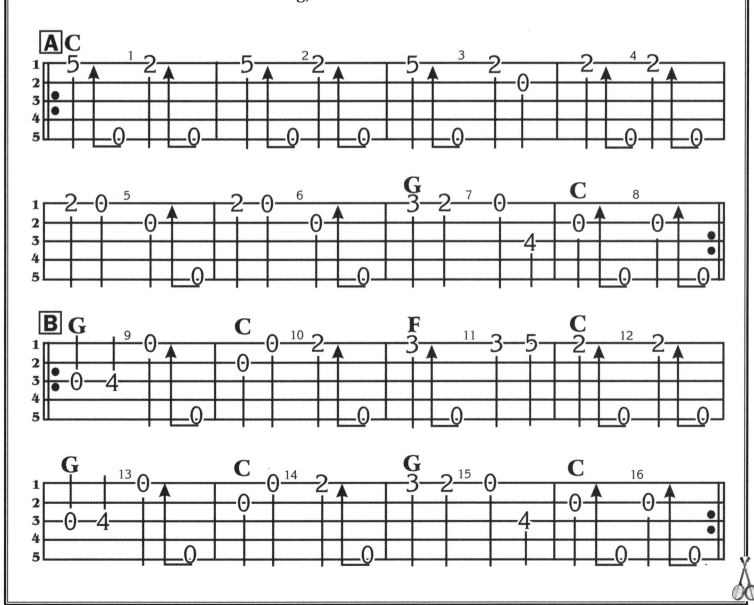

Shortenin' Bread

How many tunes can you think of that are as fun to eat as they are to play? The origins of "Shortenin' Bread" go back before the Civil War, and it has been played in virtually every musical style, with the possible exception of Classical. It was first recorded in February 1924 by Henry Whitter. Other old-time versions were recorded by Gid Tanner & His Skillet Lickers, Jackson Pavey & His Corn Shuckers, Dykes' Magic City Trio, Earl Johnson & His Dixie Entertainers, the Carter Family and J.E. Mainer's Mountaineers. Further afield, "Shortenin' Bread" has been recorded by the Beach Boys, The Andrews Sisters, Tommy Dorsey, Fats Waller, Dave Brubeck, The Ding Dong Daddies and Mississippi John Hurt.

I don't know why, but I find the melody of "Shortenin' Bread" strangely addicting. Maybe the repetition puts me into a trance (or a stupor). It's a good thing that the repetition makes it easy to learn and play.

Hot Lick #1. "Shortenin' Bread" mainly consists of single melody notes and not many clawhammers. On this kind of a tune, I would use a lot of thumbing. That means adding the 5th string after any of the single melody notes.

Hot Lick #2. To give the song some oomph, you can whack a C chord on the first beat of any or all measures. Let me explain. Hold down a C chord (1st string, 2nd fret). Instead of playing the first melody note in measures 1, 2 and 3, simply strum (or whack) down on the bottom three or four strings while holding down the C chord. Do the same thing in measure 4. On line two, the 1st string 10 fret is also a C, so you can whack the 1st string, 10th fret.

Hot Lick #3. Because "Shortenin' Bread" has strong African-American roots, it's appropriate for there to be a strong up-beat when you play it. Let me show you what I mean. As you sing or play line 1, you should tap your foot. On "Mama," your foot will hit the floor (this is called the down-beat). On "little," your foot will come up. (This is called the up-beat). So if you want to accent the up-beat throughout the entire song, you would accent every other note, starting with the first note. To accent a note means to play it harder or louder. I'll illustrate this by bolding every other word.

Mama's **little** baby **loves** shorte**nin'**, shorte**nin'**,
Mama's **little** baby **loves** shorte**nin'** bread.

How can you make a million dollars as a banjo player? *Start with two million.*

Shortenin' Bread

gCGCD - Key of C

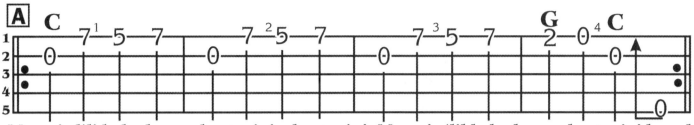

Mama's lil' baby loves shortenin', shortenin', Mama's 'lil baby loves shortenin' bread.

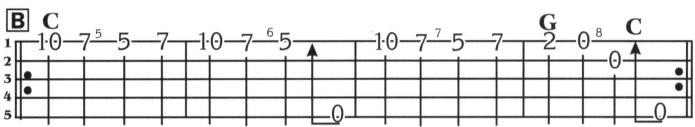

Put on the skil - let, put on the lid, Mama's gonna make a lil' shortenin' bread.
That ain't all she's gonna do, Mama's gonna make a little coffee too.

Mama's lil' baby loves shortenin', shortenin',
Mama's lil' baby loves shortenin' bread.
Mama's lil' baby loves shortenin', shortenin',
Mama's lil' baby loves shortenin' bread.

Put on the skillet, put on the lid,
Mama's gonna make a little shortenin' bread.
That ain't all she's gonna do,
Mama's gonna make a little coffee too.

Three little boys, lying in bed,
Two was sick, and the other most dead.
Sent for the doctor, and the doctor said,
"Feed them babies on shortenin' bread."

Slipped in the kitchen, slipped on the lid.
Slipped my pockets full of shortenin' bread.
Stole the skillet, stole the lid,
Stole the gal to make shortenin' bread.

I saw a guy tossing tambourines into a dumpster and I asked him why he was doing it.
"I'm getting rid of these banjo eggs before they hatch!"

Soldier's Joy

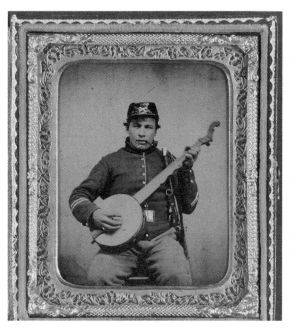

You won't be lonesome if you can play even a passable version of "Soldier's Joy." That's because it has remained one of the most popular old-time fiddle tunes for over two hundred years. Everybody knows it. And now you will too. It first made its appearance on the printed page in London in the 1770s and quickly migrated to Scotland and Ireland. Versions of the tune later showed up in Denmark, Scandinavia and even the French Alps. Soon after arriving on America's shores, it appeared in print in Benjamin and Joseph Carr's "Evening Amusement" (Philadelphia, 1796). Over its long and illustrious career, the tune has been known as "The King's Head," "The King's Hornpipe" and "Payday in the Army." Tommy Jarrell, who learned it in 1920, simply called it "Love Somebody."

Hot Lick #1. In measures 1, 3 and 5 I would add one or two slides. Fret the 4th string, 3rd fret and slide into one or both of the 4th frets on the 4th string.

Hot Lick #2. You can throw in a pull-off in measures 7 and/or 15 on the 1st string, 2nd fret.

Hot Lick #3. In measures 9, 11, and 13 you can do a pull-off on the 1st string, 2nd fret. After the pull-off firmly fret the 1st string, 2nd fret and then do a hammer-on to the 1st string 3rd fret.

Hot Lick #4. You can add some thumbing in measures 10 and 14. After the first two notes in those measures, simply play the 5th or thumb string really quickly.

What's the difference between a certificate of deposit and a banjo player?
The certificate of deposit eventually matures and earns some money.

Capo 2 to
play in D

Soldier's Joy

gCGCD - Key of C

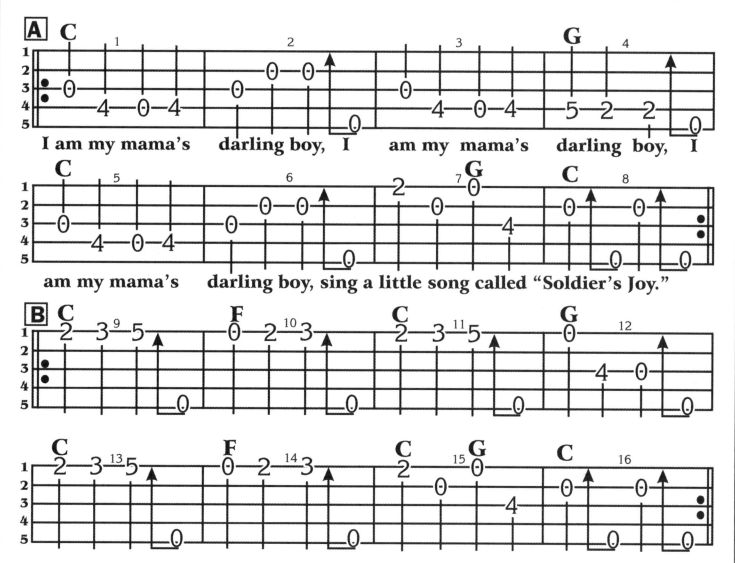

I am my mama's darling boy, I am my mama's darling boy, I

am my mama's darling boy, sing a little song called "Soldier's Joy."

Chicken in the bread pan scratching out dough,
Grannie will your dog bite, no child no,
Ladies to the center and gents catch air,
Hold her there don't let her rear.

Grasshopper sitting on a sweet potato vine,
Grasshopper sitting on a sweet potato vine,
Grasshopper sitting on a sweet potato vine,
Along come a chicken and says "You're mine!"

Twenty-five cents for the morphine,
Fifteen cents for the beer,
Twenty-five cents for the morphine,
They're gonna take me away from here.

Texas Gals

In 1963 many of us hovered over our record players and learned "Texas Gals" from an LP by Doc Watson, who played it on mandolin on "Watson Family" (Folkways FA 2366.) Doc surprised us because we weren't aware that he even played the mandolin. He later recorded it on guitar on "Ballads from Deep Gap." On both of these albums, the title is given as "Texas Gales." We are left to wonder how "Texas Gals" became "Texas Gales." It might have something to do with the fact that in the North Carolina mountains where Doc was raised, "gals" would normally be pronounced "Gales."

Doc Watson

Doc remembered that he learned "Texas Gales" from a 78 record of Al Hopkins and His Buckle Busters. On the flip side was "Going Down the Road Feeling Bad." Doc remembered that the fiddler on "Texas Gales" was Charlie Bowman. Well, I certainly hate to be the one to pop Doc Watson's balloon, but Charlie was not fiddling on "Texas Gals." Instead, it was Tony Alderson who was doing the fiddling. Doc was correct that Charlie Bowman did participate in other recordings that same day, October 22, 1926. However, it was Fred Rowe and not Charlie Bowman, who fiddled along with Tony Alderson on "Going Down the Road Feeling Bad."

My friend David Holt once asked Doc if it was "Texas Gals" or "Texas Gales." Doc joked that they're about the same, because both can be stormy.

To me, "Texas Gals" or "Gales" (whichever you prefer) sounds like three different tunes glued together. While the A part certainly sounds unique, the B part is a direct knockoff of the B part of "Billy in the Lowground." The C part of "Texas Gals" is similar to many old-time tunes, such as "Rattlesnake Bit the Baby," etc.

Hot Lick. To give this song some zing, I would add some whack-hammers to the first clawhammer lick in measures 1, 3, and 5

Chords: You can ignore the G chord in measures 1, 3, 5, 7, 12, 15, 19 and 23. Let your guitar player handle these chords. You can also ignore the F chord in measures 11 and 22. The chord that you do need to play is the C (1st string, 2nd fret).

Augusta Armstrong

Fingering: For the C part, you'll need to be somewhat athletic, because the melody jumps around like a bean on a hot skillet. In measures 17 and 21, use your ring finger or pinky to play the 4th string, 4th fret. Use this same finger in measures 18 and 22 on the 4th string, 5th fret. In measure 19, I recommend using your ring finger on the 1st string, 7th fret and your index finger to play the 1st string, 5th fret.

Texas Gals

gCGCD - Key of C

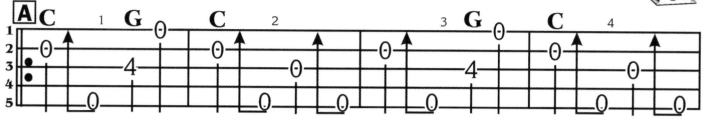

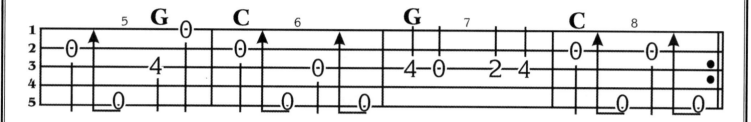

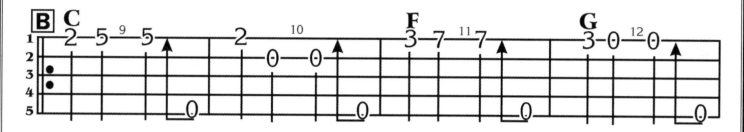

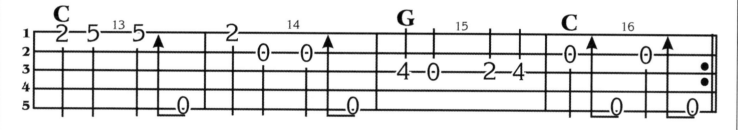

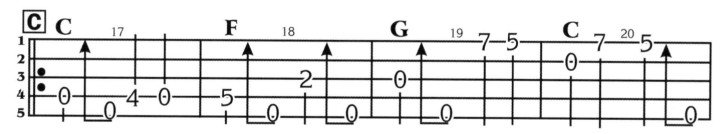

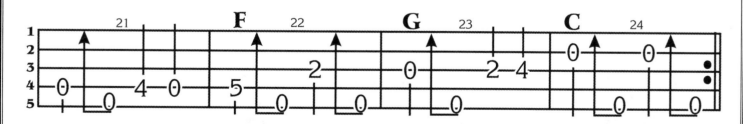

"There's just two chords on a banjo, G and not G." Stringbean

Whiskey Before Breakfast

Chasing down the history of "Whiskey Before Breakfast" is about as easy as finding the Rosetta Stone at a flea market. Thanks to the painstaking research by Andrew Kuntz and Vivian Williams, we can start to get an idea of the origins of this great old tune. There are a number of Celtic fiddle tunes such as "Greenfields of America," "Great Eastern Reel," "Bennett's Favorite" and "Silver Spire" that are suspiciously similar to the A part of "Whiskey Before Breakfast." It is likely that some variant of this family of tunes migrated to the Maritime provinces of Canada in the late 19th century, where it was known as "Spirits of the Morning." A story has been told that Canadian fiddler Andy De Jarlis and another fiddler named Houle played tunes all night until they passed out due to over lubrication with strong drink. When De Jarlis awoke, he remembered the last tune they played before passing out and named it "Whiskey Before Breakfast." In 1957, De Jarlis arranged it and included it in his book, "Canadian Fiddle Tunes from Red River Valley."

Andy DeJaris

"Whiskey Before Breakfast" was later picked up by fiddler Dick Barrett, who recorded it on a 1972 Voyager recording called "More Fiddle Jam Sessions." I remember hearing the tune in early 1972 while visiting the Seattle, Washington area, but I don't recall who was playing it. When I returned to the San Francisco Bay area, I discovered that none of my musician friends knew it, so I helped spread it around. By the mid 1970s, the tune was on everyone's "top 10" list in many parts of the country.

"Whiskey Before Breakfast" can be a very notey tune, but I've simplified it down to the bare-bones melody. (You can thank me later). To my way of thinking, a clawhammer banjo player doesn't necessarily need to always play every nuance of a tune. Instead, they should concentrate on playing the skeleton of a tune, and allow the fiddler to flesh it out.

Fingering. Be sure to use your ring or pinky finger any time the 4th string is played at the 4th or 5th fret.

Chords. As you can see, the chords hop around quite a bit on "Whiskey Before Breakfast." Of course, for the C you only need to play the 1st string, 2nd fret. For F, you can get away with only fretting the 1st string, 3rd fret. In measures 3, 7 and 15 you'll need to keep your index finger on that while you play the melody note (4th string, 5th fret) with your ring or pinky finger. To play the G chord, I like to use my middle finger on the 4th string, 2nd fret and my ring finger on the 2nd string, 2nd fret.

Capo 2 to
play in D

Whiskey Before Breakfast

33

gCGCD - Key of C

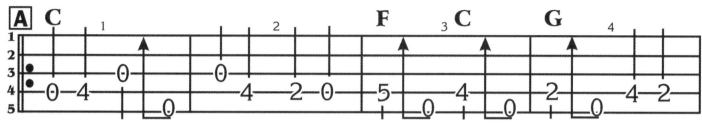

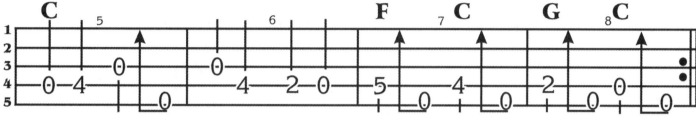

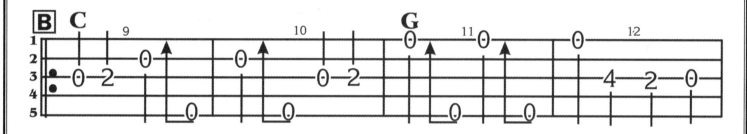

Wade Ward, 1937

45

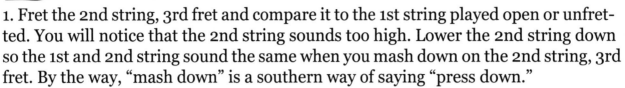

Barlow Knife

"**B**arlow Knife" will be our first tune in G tuning. The strings should be tuned to g D G B D. To go from double C tuning to G tuning, here are the steps:

1. Fret the 2nd string, 3rd fret and compare it to the 1st string played open or unfretted. You will notice that the 2nd string sounds too high. Lower the 2nd string down so the 1st and 2nd string sound the same when you mash down on the 2nd string, 3rd fret. By the way, "mash down" is a southern way of saying "press down."

2. Fret the 4th string at the 5th fret and compare it to the 3rd string played open. It should sound too low. Raise the 4th string so it matches the 3rd string played open.

Chords. As you'll soon find out, the chords to "Barlow Knife" will keep you on your toes. The G chord, however, could not be any easier. It's just an open chord, with no fingers needed. The first note of the tune (1st string, 5th fret) is part of a G chord, so when you play that first note of "Barlow Knife," all you do is mash down the 1st string, 5th fret and do your ham-mer on the open strings. When you get to the D in measure 1, you can ignore it because you'll be playing the melody without any "ham-mers" or chords. In measure 3, you should play this partial D chord when the melody is the 1st string, 4th fret.

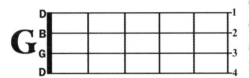

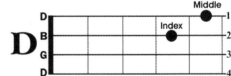

In measure 4, when the melody is on the 1st string, 2nd fret, you'll want to play this C chord. You really don't need to hit the 4th string at all, so you can forgo fingering the 4th string, 2nd fret on this C chord. However, I strongly suggest you use your ring finger on the 1st string, 2nd fret.

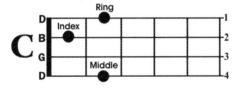

In measure 8, you'll need to play the D7 chord for one claw-ham-mer.

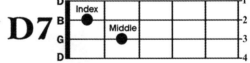

IMPORTANT: Whenever you make a chord, it is essential that all your fingers land on the strings at exactly the same time. The way to practice this is to make the chord, then lift up your fingers about 1/4 of an inch and then come down on your chord all-at-once. Make it your business to practice chords this way and you'll be a happy camper, I promise.

Hot Lick: Measures 3 and 4 are perfect places to play your drop-thumb technique that's explained on page 14.

Note: "Barlow Knife" is a three part tune. Be sure to play each part twice before going on to the next part. There are no lyrics (yet) to the C part of the tune.

Note: When you're in G tuning, D and D7 are interchangable. Feel free to use either one.

Barlow Knife

gDGBD - Key of G

One of the things I like best about old-time music is the fact that very few of the songs are the "boy meets girl, girl dumps guy" variety. Instead, they're about real stuff like hangings, getting drunk, whiskey, rabbits, chickens, getting drunk and in this case, Barlow knives. Did I mention getting drunk?

"Barlow Knife" entered the old-time repertoire from the playing of the Fuzzy Mountain String Band. The Fuzzies, as they liked to call themselves, were a loosely organized group of friends who lived in and around Durham, North Carolina. They first recorded for Rounder Records in 1971 with cobbled together equipment that was barely one step up from strings and tin cans. The LP came out just as the early 1970s revival of old-time music was clicking into gear and it was surely a factor in turning people onto this kind of music. Suddenly, it was cool to play old-time music. The core repertoire of the Fuzzies was rooted in the music of Henry Reid that they learned from their friend Alan Jabbour. Reid was from Glen Lyn, Virginia and his name for "Barlow Knife" was "Cabin Creek." Similar tunes were played in Kentucky under such names as "Blue Goose" and "I've Got a Grandpa."

At least one scholar has found traces of "Barlow Knife" going back to Scotland as early as 1627 under the title "The Old Man."

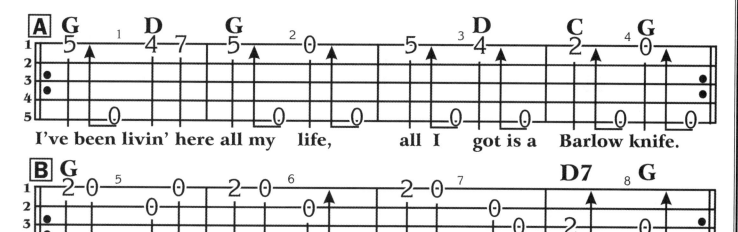

I been livin' here all my life,
All I got is a Barlow knife.
Buck horn handle and a Barlow blade,
Best dang knife that ever was made.

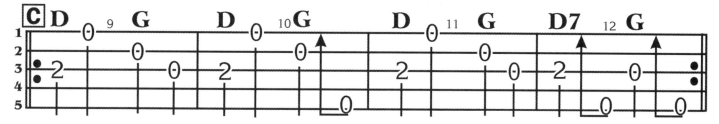

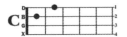

Big-Eyed Rabbit

I've recently taken quite a shine to "Big-Eyed Rabbit." Maybe this has something to do with the fact that my three kids have always kept rabbits as family pets. First we had Fuzzy, Snowy and then Bun Bun, and finally Genepy, who particularly liked the banjo. (See photo page 49). "Big-Eyed Rabbit" is currently one of the more popular tunes that you hear at many old-time jams. It was first recorded in the early 1920s by Samantha Bumgarner and Eva Davis and in the late '20s by the Stripling Brothers. The problem is that these were completely different tunes that used the same title. To confuse things even further, I have found that Matoke Slaughter and Fiddlin' Steve Ledford have each recorded completely different tunes that they also called "Big-Eyed Rabbit."

Tommy Jarrell & Fred Cockerham

The version of "Big-Eyed Rabbit" that I have written out for you is the one that was played by Tommy Jarrell, Fred Cockerham and Kyle Creed. In July of 1980, I interviewed Tommy who remembered that "It was one of my daddy's old tunes. I heard daddy play that as far back as I can recollect. I don't know where he got it."

This version of "Big-Eyed Rabbit" includes a technique we haven't used before. In measure 5, we're playing what we might call "triple thumbing." There's really not much to it. After the melody note at the beginning of measure 5, you merely hit your fifth string three times in a row.

Chords: Everything about the chords to "Big-Eyed Rabbit" are totally normal except for one thing. In measures 8, 12, and 16 you'll notice the tune goes to a D7. The tune really doesn't go back to G until two measures later. However, in the measure immediately following measures 8, 12, and 16 you'll release your D7 chord and just play the strings open on the ham-mer. You'll essentially be playing a G chord one measure earlier than the other instruments. This is just one of the quirky things about the banjo. Don't you just love it?

Note: "Big-Eyed Rabbit" really has two choruses. Most people sing the "Big-eyed rabbit" chorus for most of the tune, and "Rockin' in a weary land" the last few times they play it.

How can you tell if there's a banjo player at your door?
They can't find the key, the knocking speeds up, and they don't know when to come in.

Big-Eyed Rabbit

gDGBD - Key of G

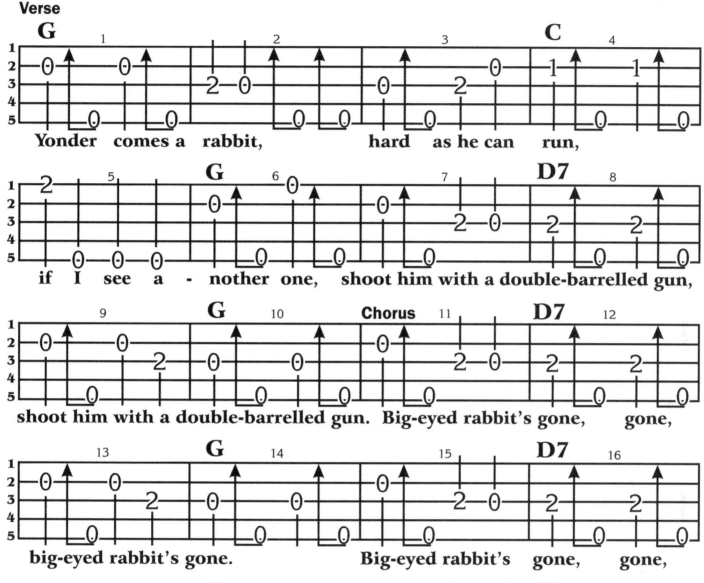

Verse

G ... **C** ...

Yonder comes a rabbit, hard as he can run,

if I see a - nother one, shoot him with a double-barrelled gun,

shoot him with a double-barrelled gun. Big-eyed rabbit's gone, gone,

big-eyed rabbit's gone. Big-eyed rabbit's gone, gone,

big-eyed rabbit's gone.

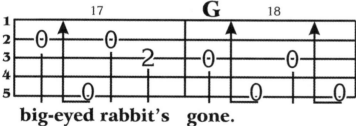

Yonder comes a rabbit,
Slippin' through the sand,
Shoot that rabbit, he don't mind,
Fry him in my pan, (2X)

Yonder comes my darlin',
And how do I know?
Know her by her pretty blue eyes,
Shinin' bright like gold, (2X)

Genepy and Gianluca De Bacco

Photo by Annie Erbsen

CHORUS:
Big-eyed rabbit's gone, gone,
Big-eyed rabbit's gone. (2X)

Rockin' in a weary land,
Rockin' in a weary land. (2X)

Dance All Night

For as long as there have been fiddlers, there have been tunes about whiskey. If you don't believe me, look at the list of only a small number of tunes about whiskey in the box, below. Commonly known as "Dance All Night With a Bottle in My Hand," this tune is strongly associated with old-time bands from Georgia, Alabama and Mississippi. First to record it was Gid Tanner and Riley Puckett on March 8. 1926. Gid Tanner recorded it again later that same year with the Skillet Lickers. Other groups that recorded it in the '20s included the Georgia Crackers (3-21-1927), the Georgia Yellow Hammers (10-24-1927), Bill Helms & His Upson County Band (2-23-1928) and the Stripling Brothers (8-19-1929).

Hot Lick. On the first clawhammer lick in measures 1, 5 and 9, you can substitute a whack-hammer.

Chords: In measure 11 of the B part, the song goes to a D while you fret the 1st string at the 7th fret. There are several ways you can play this D chord. If you like, you can cover the 1st, 2nd, 3rd and 4th strings with your index finger. This can be somewhat difficult, especially if your strings are high off the fingerboard. You'll need to apply enough pressure to make the strings ring out clear. It will help if you keep your left thumb in the middle of the back of the neck and you bend your wrist. There is a slightly easier way to play this D chord. Instead of covering four strings with your index finger, you can get by with just covering the 1st and 2nd strings. When you do your ham-mer, only hit these strings.

Fingering: On the B part of "Dance All Night" you'll be covering quite a bit of real estate. In measure 9, use your index finger to fret the 1st string, 5th fret. Then use your ring finger on the 1st string, 7th fret and your pinky for the 1st string, 9th fret. In measure 11 you'll be playing the 1st string, 7th fret on a D chord with your ring finger. For this D, I would merely add the middle finger on the 2nd string, 7th fret and do the hammer just on the bottom two strings.

Tunes About Whiskey

Humors of Whiskey, I Get My Whiskey From Rockingham, Irish Whiskey, Kentucky Whiskey, Drops of Whiskey, Niel Gow's Farewell to Whiskey, The Night the Whiskey Froze, Niel Gow's Lament for Whiskey, Ode to Whiskey, Oh Whiskey Heart of Souls, The Charms of Whiskey, Farewell Whiskey, Grand River Whiskey, How Will I Abstain From Whiskey, Little Stream of Whiskey, Drunken Hiccups, Drops of Brandy, Where'd You Get That Whiskey, Whiskey Before Breakfast, Hot Corn, Cold Corn, Rye Whiskey, Don't Sell Daddy Any More Whiskey, I Happen to Like Whiskey Sir, If The River Was Whiskey, Let Me Go Home Whiskey, Sup of Good Whiskey, There's Whiskey in the Jar, Whiskey is the Devil, Whiskey Blues, Whiskey Took My Daddy Away.

Dance All Night

gDGBD - Key of G

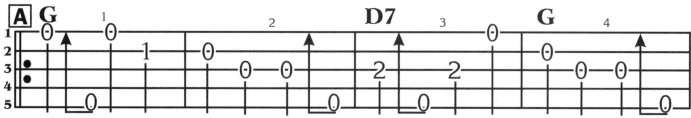

Dance all night with a bottle in my hand, a bottle in my hand, a bottle in my hand.

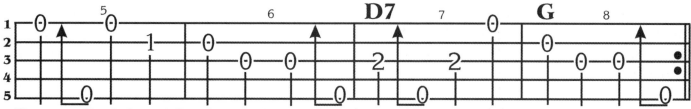

Dance all night with a bottle in my hand, just 'fore day give the fiddler a dram.

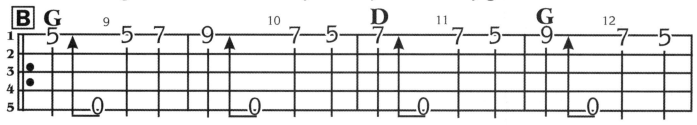

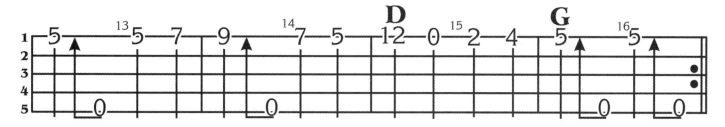

I left my jawbone sittin' on a fence,
I ain't seen nothin' of my jawbone since,
Walked on home and didn't get along,
In come Sally with her big boots on.

Who's been here since I've been gone?
Pretty little gal with the red dress on,
She took it off and I put it on,
In come Sally with her big boots on.

"Country music just never gets in my innards the way some folk music does." Guy Carawan, 1953

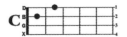

Free Little Bird

It was March, 1963. We were lucky to be at the right place at the right time as we took our seats at the Ash Grove in West Hollywood, California. As the lights dimmed and the packed audience hushed, a four-piece old-time group from North Carolina and east Tennessee took the stage. We weren't quite sure who they were, but we figured it would be good. We were right! These four gentlemen were about to turn an audience of urban folkies into die hard fans of old-time music. The musicians included Clarence "Tom" Ashley on clawhammer banjo, Doc Watson on guitar, Fred Price on fiddle and Clint Howard on second guitar (see photo, below). The music that we witnessed that night blew the hats right off our heads! Many of us had never seen or heard authentic clawhammer playing before. Of course, practically no one had ever seen the likes of Doc Watson on guitar. His rendition of "Black Mountain Rag" changed people's idea of what flatpicking guitar was all about. That night was the first time I heard "Free Little Bird."

In the years since that night, I've come to learn that it has been a very popular tune going back at least to the mid 1920s. First to record it was Land Norris in July of 1925, followed by John Hammond, Dykes' Magic City Trio, The Allen Brothers, Rutherford & Foster and Ridgel's Fountain Citians.

The Key. Because "Free Little Bird" is a song, rather than a tune, we can play it in any key that suits our fancy. I've written it out for you in the key of C because this seems to be a key where many people sing it. The one thing that's somewhat unusual about this arrangement is that we'll be playing it in the key of C, but in G tuning. I'm doing this to show that you often do not have to change tuning to double C tuning to play in the key of C. You can do all of your noting and chording right in G tuning. What's the point in doing it this way? To make you more versatile. If you get used to playing C tunes out of G tuning, you're suddenly able to switch from the key of G to the key of C without breaking a sweat. This will be handy when you're playing in a jam.

Chords: When I make a C chord in G tuning, I normally just use two fingers. Be sure to use your ring finger on the 1st string. This will make your middle finger available to fret the 4th string, 2nd fret should the need arise.

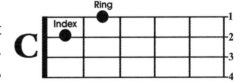

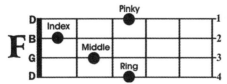

This is a good F position to use. It's almost like the D7 chord, with the addition of your pinky on the 1st string, 3rd fret and your ring finger on the 4th string, 3rd fret. **Note**: unless you plan to hit the 4th string when you do the clawhammer, you can leave your ring finger off.

Hot Lick: You can add a hammer-on in measures 2, 6 and 10 when the melody is on the 1st string, 2nd fret followed by a ham-mer.

Free Little Bird

gDGBD - Key of C

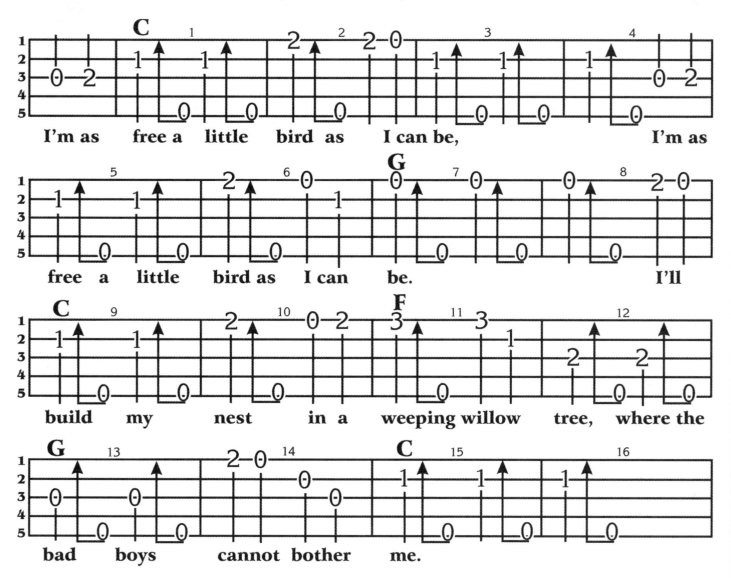

I'm as free a little bird as I can be,
I'm as free little bird as I can be.
I'm as free at my age as a bird in the cage,
I'm as free a little bird as I can be.

Oh, I'll never build my nest on the ground,
Oh, I'll never build my nest on the ground,
But I'll build my nest in a weeping willow tree,
Where the bad boys cannot tear me down.

Oh, I'll never steal honey from a tree,
I'll never steal honey from a tree,
But I'll steal me a kiss from my sweet darling's lips,
And fly away across the sea.

53

Georgia Railroad

D7

Long before Nashville became known as the center of the country music industry, New York City was the place to go to make records. In early September of 1924, Gid Tanner and Riley Puckett journeyed from Atlanta, Georgia to the Columbia Records studio in New York City. Among their first recordings was a tune they called "Georgia Railroad." Later that year it was recorded by Fiddlin' John Carson as "Peter Went A-Fishing." More recently, it has been recorded by Norman and Nancy Blake, The Possum Hunters, the Ledford Stringband, the Foghorn Stringband and the Locust Honey Stringband.

For all you fishermen, a mudcat is a species of bullhead catfish found in the Mississippi Delta. They're typically not a huge fish, but are "frying size," as my dad used to say.

Hot Lick #1. Instead of playing the first two melody notes in measures 1 and 5 as written, you can slide into these notes. Fret the 3rd string at the 2nd fret and then slide up to the 4th fret. Instead of just hitting the 3rd string by itself, you can get a bigger sound by whacking on the 1st, 2nd and 3rd strings at the same time you do the slide. Of course, after the slide you'll need to do a quick ham-mer. The slide with the clawhammer should sound like "slide-ham-mer."

Jupiter & Lake Worth Railroad, 1896

Photo by William Henry Jackson

Note: In the B part, there's several cool pull-offs you'll want to play. In measures 9 and 13, fret the 1st string at the 5th fret with your ring finger and play that note. Then you'll move down and fret the 1st string, 4th fret again with your ring finger AND the 1st string, 2nd fret with your index finger. Do a pull-off on the 1st string, 4th fret while continuing to hold your index finger on the 1st string, 2nd fret.

Hot Lick #2. If you'd like to add more accent to "Georgia Railroad," you can whack the first note in measures 9 and 11.

Another Note: In measures 10 and 14 you'll find another pull-off. This one is a little easier, because you'll be pulling-off to an open string.

Chords: The first note in measures 4 and 12 is the 2nd string open followed by a ham-mer. Even though the song stays on a D7 chord right there, you can lift up your fingers off the D7 to play the clawhammer lick.

Georgia Railroad

gDGBD - Key of G

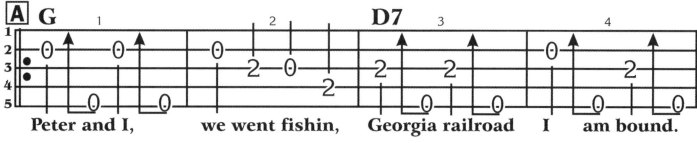

Peter and I,   we went fishin,   Georgia railroad   I   am bound.

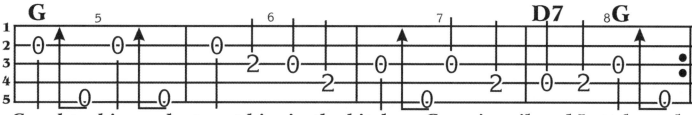

Caught a big mudcat, put him in the kitchen, Georgia railroad I am bound.

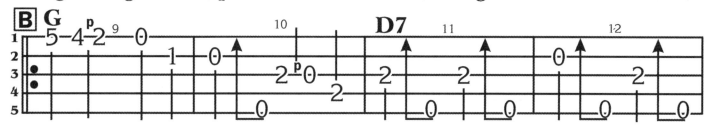

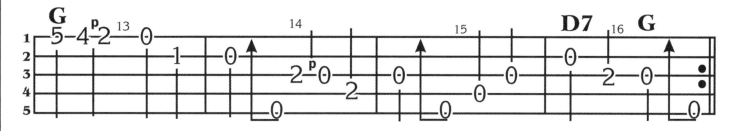

Peter and I, we went fishin',
Georgia railroad I am bound.
Caught a big mud-cat put him in the kitchen,
Georgia railroad I am bound.

Walked down the road 'til it got right muddy,
Georgia railroad I am bound,
But I'm so drunk I can't stand steady,
Georgia railroad I am bound.

I got drunk and fell in a gully,
Georgia railroad I am bound.
I got drunk but I never got muddy,
Georgia railroad I am bound.

Photo by Wayne Erbsen

What's the best way to tune a banjo? *With wire cutters.*

55

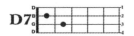

Hangman's Reel

I'm always reminded of my old friend and mentor, Albert Hash when I think of "Hangman's Reel." I first met Albert at the Grayson County Fiddler's Convention in the summer of 1972 and took an instant liking to him. Not only was he a great old-time fiddler, but I was drawn to him by his plain-spoken ways and his humble spirit. He spoke in an old-time Southwest Virginia dialect, and I hung on his every word. The man was wise from his head to his toes and I spent a lot of time visiting and playing music with him at his Whitetop Mountain home. His wife Ethel used to fix me instant coffee with hot water from the tap. It was delicious!

Photo by Mark Sanderford

Albert Hash

Back in the early '70s, Albert taught me "Hangman's Reel." Over the years, I'm sure I've embellished both the tune and the story that goes with it. Here's the story:

Many years ago in Canada, there was a condemned man who was nervously awaiting his execution the following day for a crime that is long forgotten. Through the cold, iron bars of his cell he could hear carpenters building his gallows. The jailhouse walls were too thick to tunnel through, so he was desperate to figure out a way to escape his fate. Looking through the bars, he could see an old fiddle hanging on the wall of the jailer's office. That gave him an idea. He called the jailer over and pretended that he was the greatest fiddle player in that entire region. After arguing back and forth, the prisoner managed to goad the jailer into making a bet. If he could prove that he was the greatest fiddler, he would be set free. But if he was lying and was not the great fiddler that he claimed to be, then he would meet his fate at the end of the hangman's rope. They shook hands and sealed the bet. The jailor allowed the prisoner to keep the fiddle and bow in his cell overnight. The next day with the noose tied neatly around his neck, he would get the chance to play fiddle for the crowd and settle the bet once and for all.

Truth was, the prisoner had never held a fiddle in his hands before, but it was the only thing he could think of to try and win his release. You can bet he stayed up late that night figuring out how to play that fiddle. On the gallows the next morning, the prisoner raised the fiddle and played the tune that has since become known as "Hangman's Reel." History did not bother to record whether the prisoner won his freedom or instead received a "suspended" sentence. However, we are left with a darn good tune!

"Hangman's Reel" is a four-part tune that doesn't need a whole lot of fancy shenanigans because

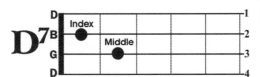

you'll have many melody notes to keep you busy. However, here's one thing you can do. In the A part you'll be going back and forth from G to D7. Instead of hitting just the melody note on one string, you can hit the 2nd and 3rd strings at the same time. After you play the D7 in measure 1, slide both of your fingers up two frets so you'll be making a D7 on the 3rd and 4th frets. This is actually a G chord. So, you can slide into your new G position as many times as you like on the A part of the tune.

Hangman's Reel

gDGBD - Key of G

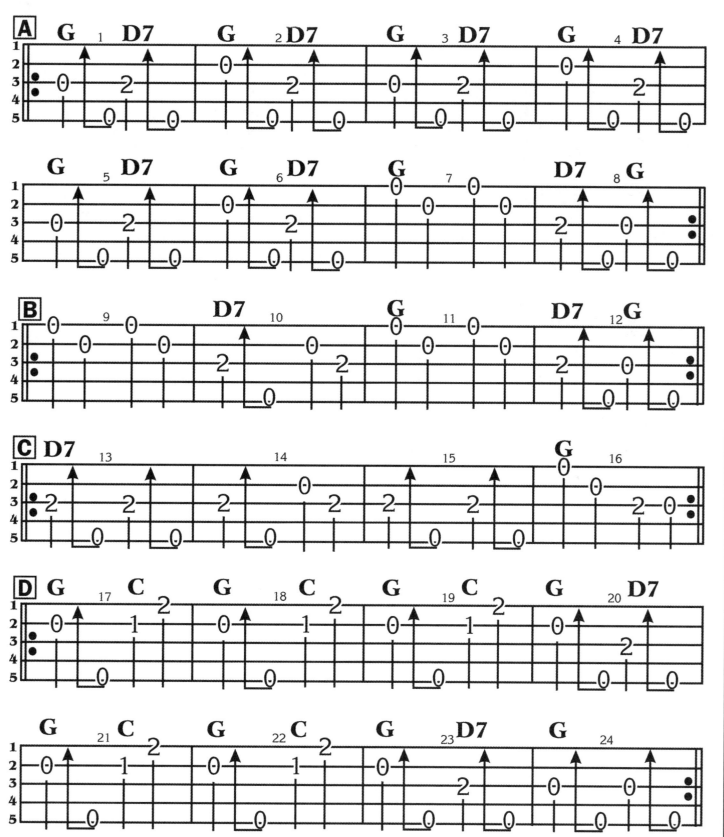

Why did the banjo player look over the chain link fence? *To see what was on the other side.*

I've Endured

Photo by Carl Fleischhauer

Ola Belle Reed

ountry music star Marty Stuart said it best when he titled his sixth studio album "This One's Gonna Hurt You." That record included one of Ola Belle Reed's best-known songs, "High on a Mountain." The same thing can be said for this Ole Belle composition, "I've Endured." She had a way of expressing deep emotion with just a few words. Both old-time and bluegrass musicians have not been shy about including this song in their repertoire. It has been recorded by the likes of Doc Watson, Mac Wiseman, Del McCoury, Tim O'Brien, the Konnarock Critters and the Wolfe Brothers.

Hot Lick #1. Instead of playing the first 5th fret in measure 1, use a slide. Merely play the 1st string at the 2nd fret and quickly slide up to the 5th fret followed by the ham-mer.

Hot Lick #2. You can also add a whack-hammer as you slide up to the 5th fret in measure 1.

Hot Lick #3. Throughout "I've Endured," you'll see numerous times when the 1st string, 2nd fret is followed by a ham-mer. To add a little variety, you can do a hammer-on to some of those notes.

Hot Lick #4. Instead of playing the 2nd string open followed by a ham-mer in measures 9, 10, 14 and 15, you can add a slide. Fret the 3rd string, 2nd fret and slide up to the 4th fret.

Barefoot in the summer on into the fall,
Too many mouths to feed they couldn't clothe us all,
Sent to church on Sunday to learn the golden rule,
I've endured, I've endured, how long can one endure?

I've worked for the rich, I've lived with the poor,
I've seen many a heartache there'll be many a more,
I've lived, loved and sorrowed, been to success's door,
I've endured, I've endured, how long can one endure?

How do you get a banjo player's eyes to sparkle? *Shine a light in his/her ears.*

I've Endured

By Ola Belle Reed © Midstream Music (BMI)

gDGBD - Key of G

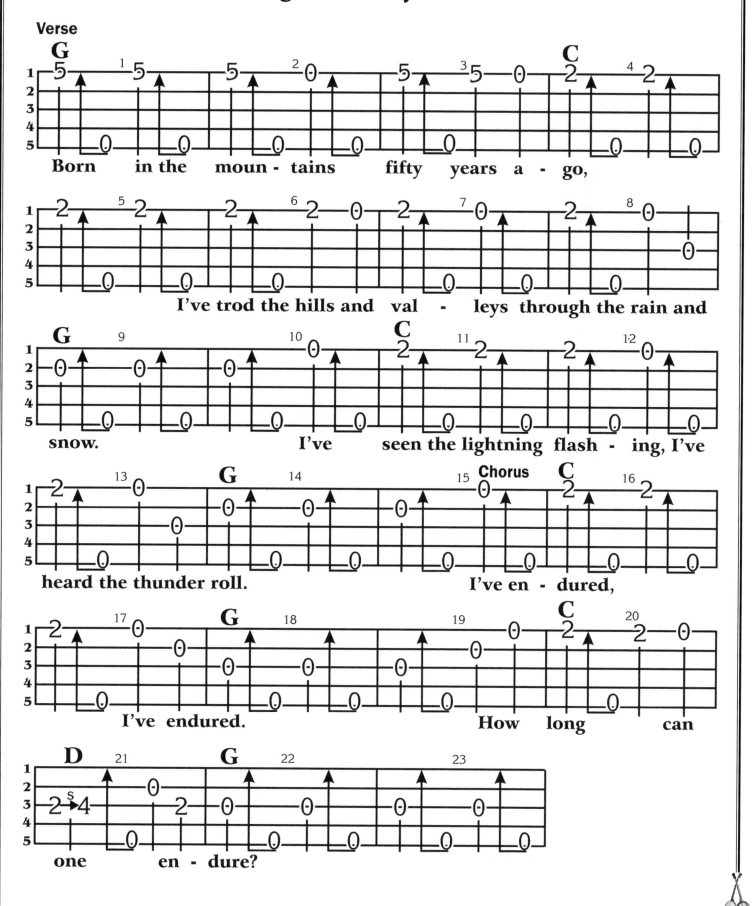

Lazy John

D7 chord diagram

C chord diagram

Over the years there's been a number of different old-time songs called "Lazy John." Jean Ritchie from Viper, Kentucky and Morris Norton from Madison County, North Carolina each did their own version of a song they called "Lazy John." The source of this "Lazy John" was Clyde Davenport from Monticello, Kentucky. Clyde remembers learning it off the radio, possibly from Johnnie Lee Wills, Bob Wills' brother. In recent years, it has been recorded by April Verch, Mike Compton/Joe Newberry, Paul Brown, Tim Gardner, Chance McCoy, Bruce Molsky and many more too numerous to mention. Brad Leftwich and Linda Higginbotham collaborated in adding the last two verses and recorded them on a 1996 album called "Say Old Man." Thanks, Brad and Linda!

Hot Lick #1. Hammer-ons are a good way to decorate "Lazy John." Any time the melody is on any string at the 2nd fret, you can do a hammer-on. I count 22 times the melody is on the 2nd fret. So for any of these notes, you can do a hammer-on. Of course, you wouldn't want to hammer on all of them!

Hot Lick #2. In measures 2 and 6 the melody is the 2nd string open followed by a ham-mer. Instead of playing the 2nd string open, you can fret the 3rd string at the 2nd fret and slide up to the 4th fret. Then, quickly play your ham-mer.

Photo by Carl Fleischhauer

Lee Hammons

Lazy John

gDGBD - Key of G

Verse

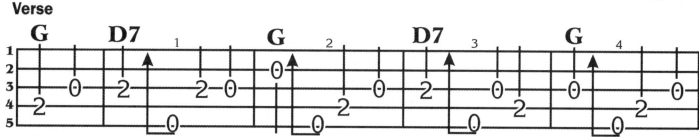

I've got a gal, she lives by the road, her eyes are crooked, and her legs are bowed, but she

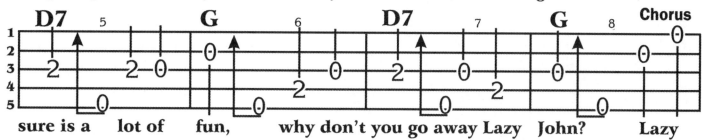

sure is a   lot of   fun,   why don't you go away Lazy   John?   **Chorus** Lazy

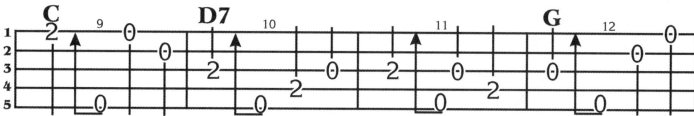

John, Lazy John, why don't you get your day's work all done? You're in the

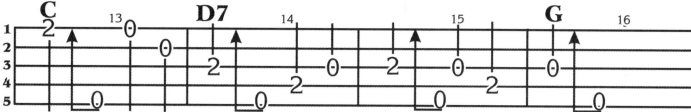

shade, and I'm in the sun, why don't you go away Lazy John?

Lazy John, Lazy John,
Why don't you get your day's work all done?
You're in the shade, I'm in the sun,
Why don't you go away Lazy John?

Every night when I get home,
It's peas in the pot and an old jawbone,
Here today but tomorrow he's gone,
Why don't you get away lazy John?

I'm going to the dance on Saturday night,
We're gonna dance 'til the broad daylight,
Then I'll take my sweetie back home,
Why don't you go away Lazy John?

I work all week in the noonday sun,
It's fifteen cents when Saturday comes,
Going to the dance to have some fun,
Why don't you get away lazy John?

Samantha Bumgarner

Let Me Fall

Many of us learned "Let Me Fall" directly from Tommy Jarrell himself, who explained to me in July of 1980 how he got to playing it. "I learned that song from Charlie Lowe, my daddy-in-law, way up on the mountain up yonder. He called it 'Let Me Fall.' I never heard my daddy play it until he got to playin' it that night with my daddy-in-law. We were up there two or three weeks making whiskey. We got to playing it that night. It was the first time I'd heard my daddy play it."

Hot Lick #1. You can do a pull-off on the 2nd string, 1st fret, which is the second note of "Let Me Fall." You can do the pull-off again on the "1" in measure 5.

Hot Lick #2. Immediately after you do this pull-off, you can do a slide on the 2nd string, 1st fret up to the 2nd string, 3rd fret to take the place of the 1st string open.

Hot Lick #3. You can try some thumbing in measure 4. Immediately after you play the 3rd fret in measure 4, hit the 5th string with your thumb.

Hot Lick #4. In measure 3 you can occasionally add a hammer-on to the 2nd string, 1st fret.

Joy ride, 1924

"My daddy always used to say that music was supposed to roll just like a wheel — the same speed all the time. If you start out fast, keep it a-going. If you start out slow or medium, keep it a-rolling. Don't play fast and then slow." Tommy Jarrell

Let Me Fall

gDGBD - Key of G

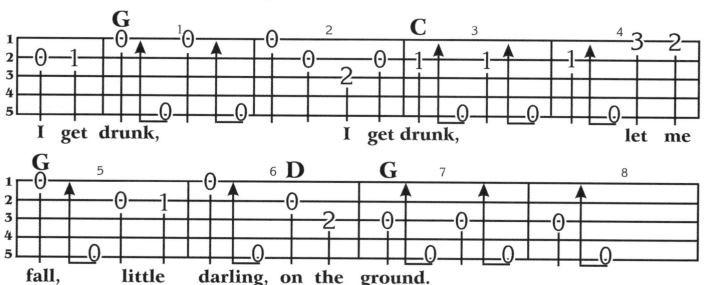

I get drunk,   I get drunk,   let me

fall,   little   darling, on the ground.

Oh hard road, Oh hard road,
Kill me dead, kill me dead, kill me dead.

I get drunk, I get drunk,
Let me fall, little darling on the ground.

Oh me, oh my,
Let me fall, little darling, let me fall.

Weep and moan, weep and moan,
Carry me home, little darling, carry me home.

Tie my shoes, tie my shoes,
Tie my shoes, little darling, tie my shoes.

Tommy Jarrell and Bill Hicks, Union Grove, NC

Tommy Jarrell's Proposal of Marriage

You can learn a lot about Tommy by the way he proposed to his wife, Nina. They had known each other for about two years when he proposed to her while they were both hoeing corn one day. "Nina, we'll get married if you want to. But I'll tell you right now, I make whiskey, I play poker, and I go to dances, make music, and I don't know whether I'll ever quit that or not. But, if you think we can get along now, we'll get married — and if you don't think we can, right now's the time to say something." Nina said, "Well, I believe we'd get along all right."

Puncheon Floor

There are at least two other tunes with the title "Puncheon Floor," but I'll bet this is the only one that changes keys in the middle. Just so you'll know, a puncheon floor was used in the earliest log cabins on the frontier. Before sawmills became widespread, there was no practical way to get lumber to build the floor of a cabin. As a substitute for lumber, logs were split lengthwise using steel or locust wedges and were then dressed using a broadaxe and an adze. When laid side-by-side, the flat side of the split logs became the new floor of the cabin.

Even though "Puncheon Floor" is undoubtedly an old tune, I cannot find any versions that were commercially recorded in the 1920s or 30s. However, musicologist Andrew Kuntz has managed to trace the earliest version of "Puncheon Floor" to a fiddler by the name of Crawley Hamlin from Dobson, North Carolina.

You will find the A part of "Puncheon Floor" quite straight forward and easy. However, the B part is a mess! First, it abruptly changes to the key of D, and then the melody hops all over the place. Your fingers will need to be quite nimble to play the B part up to speed.

Noting. Whenever the melody is on the 1st string, 5th fret such as in measures 3 and 4, you can simply play the 5th string open.

Fingering. Let me give you some suggestions on what fingers to use on the B part of "Puncheon Floor." In measure 9, use your pinky to play the 1st string at the 7th fret. Use your index or middle finger on the 1st string, 4th fret. On the 1st string, 5th fret, you can use your middle or ring finger. Any time the melody is on the 1st string, 2nd fret be sure to use your index finger. And when the melody goes to the 1st string, 4th fret, use your ring finger. No matter what fingers you use you'll have to hustle to get to all these notes quick enough.

The clawhammer rhythm. On the B part, the notes come in such a rapid-fire manner that it's really not practical to play the chords while you play the melody. Instead, on any of the notes that have the "ham-mer," simply do the "ham-mer" only on the melody note.

The ending. After you've played the tune umpteen times and you're ready to quit, you'll need to play the A part two more times after the B part.

Hot Lick. In the B part, there are several accents you can use to give the tune some dynamics. When there's an A chord in measures 10, 11, 12, and 14 make the A chord by covering the 1st and 2nd strings with your left index finger. Instead of playing the melody note on the 1st string as written, whack both the notes you're holding down with your finger. We call this the "whack-hammer." Encourage your guitar player to accent his or her A chord with yours and you're sure to win a banjo contest with this one.

> Joe: "My car was broken into yesterday and I had my banjo on the back seat."
> Jack: "Did they take it?" Joe: *"No, but they left me two more banjos."*

Puncheon Floor

gDGBD - Keys of G & D

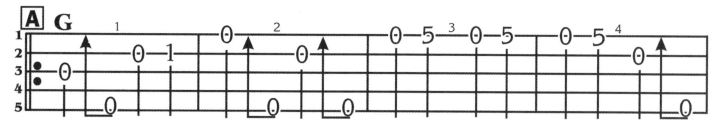

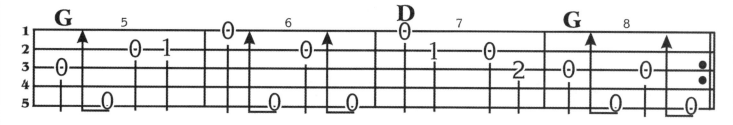

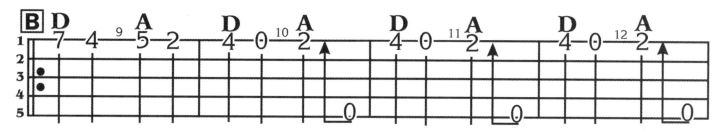

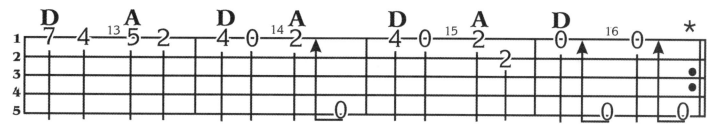

* Play A part twice.

Sad-Eyed Sadie

By Wayne Erbsen © 2015 Fracas Music (BMI)
gDGBD - Key of E Minor

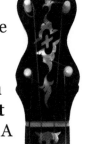

On this spooky tune you can ignore all the D chords and also the B7 in measure 8. The "P" in measures 6 and 8 means pull-off (page 13).

Hot Lick #1: If you'd like to add a little drama to this tune, stop suddenly after you play the first note in measure 16. Start up again at the beginning of the A part. **Hot Lick #2:** You can add hammer-ons in measures 9, 11, 12 and 13. **Note:** Play the A part twice, the B part once, then the A part once.

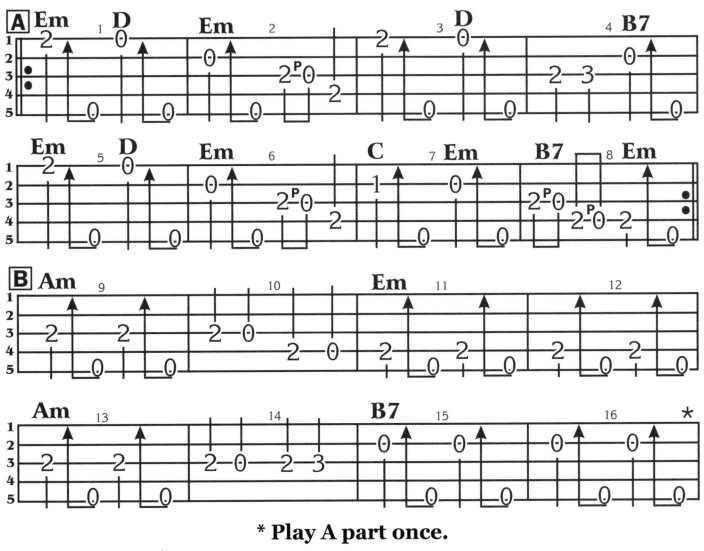

* Play A part once.

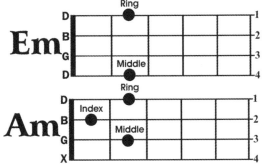

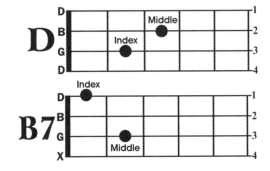

Seneca Square Dance

46

gDGBD - Key of G

Growing up in California, I was lucky enough to learn this tune at the knee of legendary blind mandolin and fiddle player, Kenny Hall. When you learned a tune from Kenny, you knew you learned it *right* because he was a no-nonsense kind of musician who played clear and bedrock versions of tunes. Any time we were around Kenny, we felt like we were learning from the horse's mouth, so to speak. *Seneca Square Dance* has a long and twisted history that goes back at least to the Civil War. It has gone under such names as *Waiting For the Federals, Higher Up the Monkey Climbs, Got a Little Home to Go To* and *Shelby's Mules* (named after Confederate cavalry commander General Joseph Shelby).

This tune is pretty straightforward. At the beginning of measure 13, fret the 1st, 2nd and 3rd strings at the 5th fret to make the C.

Hot Lick. In measure 1, 3 and 5 you can replace the 2nd string open with the clawhammer with a slide from the 3rd string, 2nd fret to the 4th fret.

Kenny Hall

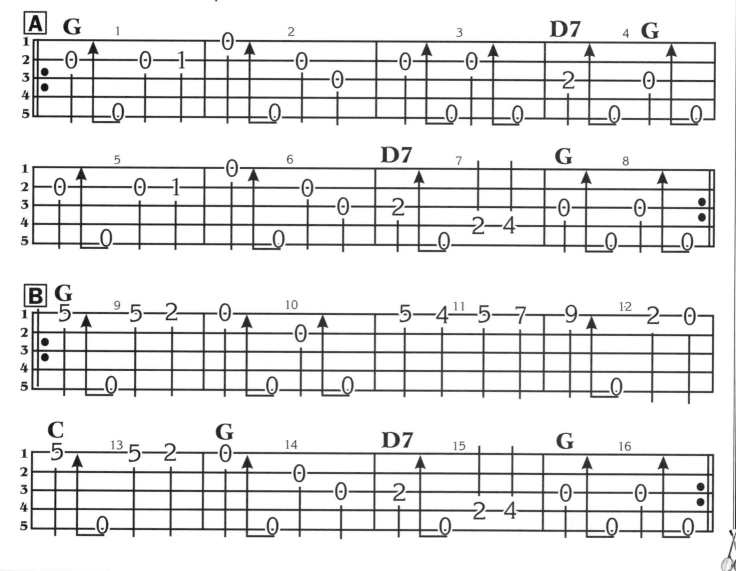

Stay All Night

Library of Congress

Happy John

This rollicking tune seems to have its origin in Grayson County, Virginia and nearby Surry County, North Carolina. It is now commonly called "Waterbound," but it was first recorded as "Way Down in North Carolina" on March 3, 1929 by Fields Ward & The Grayson County Railsplitters. Tommy Jarrell and Fred Cockerham recorded it in 1973 for County Records with the title, "Stay All Night." The main difference between the Fields Ward and the Tommy and Fred version is that Tommy and Fred go to a C chord in the B part. My way of playing it is largely based on the Tommy and Fred version. Although it's commonly played in the key of A, you should play "Stay All Night" in any key that suits your voice.

Hot Lick #1. There are several places you can add hammer-ons such as in measure 3, when the melody is on the 3rd string, 2nd fret followed by a ham-mer.

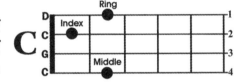

Hot Lick #2. You can give that C chord at the beginning of measure 9 more punch by doing a whack-ham-mer instead of the first clawhammer. You can use this complete C chord or the partial C chord shown above.

Hot Lick #3. If you really want to get fancy on the first clawhammer lick in measure 9, you can hammer-on an entire C chord. All you do is whack all the strings and then hammer down the full C chord.

Hot Lick #4. In measures 10, 11, 14 and 15 you can put in some thumbing. After any of the single notes (without a clawhammer), play the 5th string really quick.

Chords. At the end of measure 10, the melody is on the 1st string, 5th fret. Use your ring finger to make that note. Then add your middle finger on the 2nd string, 5th fret, and do your clawhammer on the 1st and 2nd strings. This will give you the sound of a C chord.

The two gentlemen seated in the weathered photo on the facing page are Friel and Houston Galyean. The story has been passed down through the family that Houston Galyean was killed in 1904. He had apparently passed out drunk in the middle of the road sometime before old man Charlie Smith came around the curve driving a team of oxen pulling a wagon load of tanning bark headed for Mount Airy, North Carolina. With Charlie unable to stop his team, Galyean was killed when the wagon ran over him. If Charlie had been driving a team of horses, local folks are convinced that the horses would have shied away from running over poor Houston, but the oxen did not stop.

Stay All Night

gDGBD - Key of G

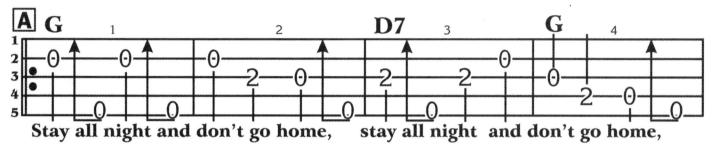

Stay all night and don't go home,   stay all night and don't go home,

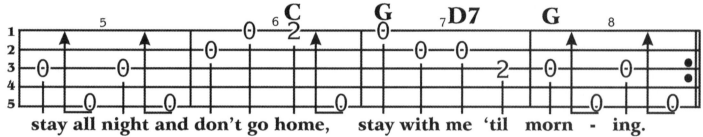

stay all night and don't go home,   stay with me 'til morn - ing.

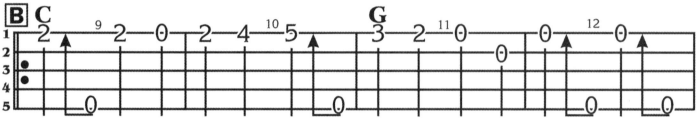

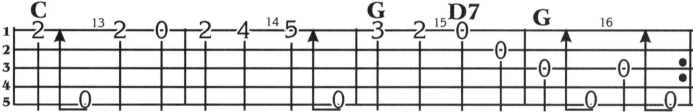

River's up and I can't get across,
River's up and I can't get across,
River's up and I can't get across,
Stay with me 'til morning.

Give five dollars for an old blind horse,
Give five dollars for an old blind horse,
He fell down and I've got to get across.
Stay with me 'til morning.

I kicked and I spurred and I couldn't get him in,
I kicked and I spurred and I couldn't get him in,
Give five dollars to take him back again,
Stay with me 'til morning.

Photo courtesy of Teresa Smith

Friel Galyean (l), Houston Gaylean (r)

69

Sugar in the Gourd

Without a doubt, "Sugar in the Gourd" is one of the oldest tunes in this book. It very well could have come from Scotland, Ireland or England because scores of tunes from the British Isles bear traces of it. Musicologist Charles Wolfe found copies of the lyrics dating back to the 1830s. It may have come from the same family of tunes that produced "Old Zip Coon," and "Turkey in the Straw." Numerous floating verses have often attached to it, including the two verses below the tab, which are also sometimes found in several Civil War songs such as "There Was An Old Soldier," "The Old Soldier With The Wooden Leg," or "The Old Tobacco Box."

Most fiddlers like Gid Tanner, Clayton McMichen and Fiddlin' John Carson played "Sugar in the Gourd" in the key of A, but others such as Fiddlin' Powers played it in the key of E. Norman Edmonds played a completely different tune in E that he called "Sugar in the Gourd."

Courtesy of Appalshop

Morgan Sexton

As usual, I've tabbed out the bare-naked skeleton of the tune. Try any or all of these hot licks to dress the skeleton.

Hot Lick #1. You can add a hammer-on in measures 1 and 2. Play the 3rd string open and then quickly hammer onto the 3rd string, 2nd fret. Then play the 2nd string open and hammer onto the 2nd string, 1st fret.

Hot Lick #2. Instead of playing the clawhammer at the beginning of measure 3, you can replace it with a pull-off. All you do is play the 1st string, 2nd fret, and pull that off to the open 1st string. Quickly follow the pull-off with the 2nd string, 1st fret.

Hot Lick #3. In measure 4, instead of playing the 2nd string open, you can add a hammer-on. Simply play the 2nd string open, and then hammer down on the 2nd string, 1st fret.

Hot Lick #4. In measure 5, do a whack-hammer instead of the first clawhammer.

Hot Lick #5. In measures 9 and 11 you'll notice the 4th string open is followed by the 3rd string open. Instead of playing these notes this way, you can substitute the 4th string open with a hammer-on at the 2nd fret of the 4th string.

Q. How many banjo players does it take to screw in a light bulb?
A. *Five. One to screw it in and four to lament that they don't make them like they used to.*

Sugar in the Gourd

gDGBD - Key of G

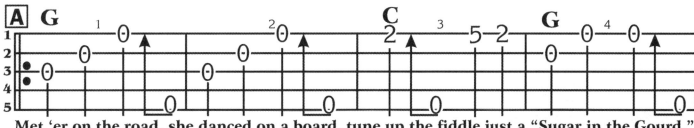

Met 'er on the road, she danced on a board, tune up the fiddle just a "Sugar in the Gourd."

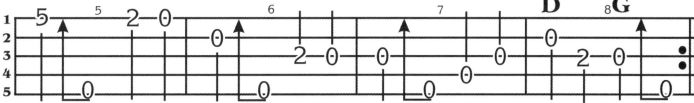

Sugar in the Gourd 'n I can't get it out, way to get the sugar out is to roll the gourd about.

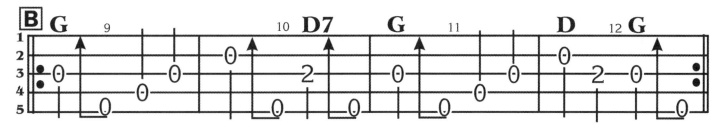

I had a little hen and she had a wooden leg,
Best dern hen that ever laid an egg,
Laid more eggs than any hen around the farm,
Another little drink wouldn't do me any harm.

Oh, I had a little duck and she had a web foot,
She built her nest in a mulberry root,
She ruffled up her feathers to keep herself warm,
Another little drink would help me along.

I went down in the old clay field,
Blacksnake grabbed me by the heel,
I turned around to do my best,
And drove my head in a hornet's nest.

Some folks say that a preacher won't steal,
But I caught three in my cornfield,
One had a bushel and one had a peck,
One had a roastin' ear around his neck.

Chilly Winds

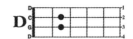

Wade Ward

Here is a true folk tune in that it draws from a number of diverse sources. The melody seems to be based on the same form as "John Henry," and some of the lyrics are shared by such songs as "Lonesome Road Blues," or "Goin' Down the Road Feelin' Bad" and "Hello Stranger," as done by the Carter Family. It's interesting to note that Wade Ward, who lived near Independence, Virginia, played a different tune he called "Chilly Winds," which bears a close resemblance to "Lonesome Road Blues," but is an instrumental.

This version of "Chilly Winds" comes to us from Tommy Jarrell. In talking with Mike Seeger about "Chilly Winds," Tommy recalled that "I thought it was the prettiest thing I ever heard." In that same conversation, Tommy told how he learned "Chilly Winds."

"Carlie Holder and me was playing for a dance when I was about fifteen or sixteen years old—I was just beginning to play the fiddle....back then you didn't have over six or eight girls, you know, and they'd get tired and want to rest a while. While they was a-resting, why Carlie, he got to playing that tune, the first time I ever heard it. Then I got him to play it a right smart little bit, maybe over two or three times and I learned it right there. I was young then, I could listen to a fellow play a tune, you know, and it would go in my head and stay. And I used to know a lot of words to it but I forgot 'em cause I quit making music for about forty years there. I didn't play none much and I forgot some of them songs."

This helps to explain why on Tommy's recording of "Chilly Winds," he didn't sing all the words. Instead, he only sang a few fragments such as "I'll see you when your troubles are like mine, I'll see you when you haven't got a dime" and "I'm goin' where the chilly winds don't blow, I'm going where the climate suits my clothes." In the 1980s, the old-time group The Renegades made a complete song out of it by borrowing some additional words from "Lonesome Road Blues."

Sawmill Tuning. "Chilly Winds" is the first of six tunes in what Clarence "Tom" Ashley called sawmill tuning. It's basically G tuning with the 2nd or B string tuned up one fret from B to C. All you do is fret the 2nd string at the 2nd fret and tune up the 2nd string so it matches the 1st string open. The notes are gDGCD. **Note:** Any time you're clawhammering on the 3rd string open, you can either ignore the G chord or play the 2nd string, 2nd fret. The D chord is shown above.

Chilly Winds Tuning. This is totally optional, but if you like, you can tune the D or 4th string way down to a low G note. Fret the 4th string at the 12 fret, and make it sound like the 3rd string open.

Hot Lick. I would add a whack-hamm-er on the first clawhammer in measures 1, 5, and 9. If you've got reasonably long fingers, you can keep your index finger on the 2nd string, 2nd fret and your pinky on the 1st string, 5th fret when you do the whack-ham-mer.

Chilly Winds

gDGCD - Key of G Modal

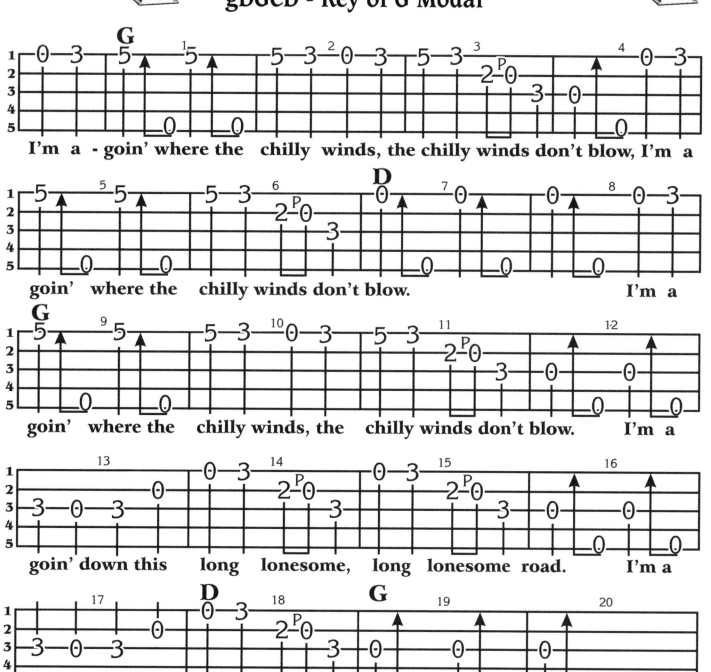

I'm a - goin' where the chilly winds, the chilly winds don't blow, I'm a

goin' where the chilly winds don't blow. I'm a

goin' where the chilly winds, the chilly winds don't blow. I'm a

goin' down this long lonesome, long lonesome road. I'm a

goin' down this long, lonesome road.

I'm goin' where the climate suits, the climate suits my clothes,
I'm goin' where the climate suits my clothes.
I'm goin' where the climate suits, the climate suits my clothes,
I'm goin' down this long lonesome, long lonesome road,
I'm goin' down this long lonesome road.

I'm goin' where the water tastes, the water tastes like wine....

Greasy Coat

Edden Hammons

Sometimes called "Old Greasy Coat," this West Virginia tune can be traced directly back to Edden Hammons. Growing up in the 1870s in Webster County, West Virginia in a family of fiddlers, Edden's extraordinary skill on the fiddle was noticed even as a young boy. Because of his musical gifts, his parents hopelessly pampered him and excused him from doing any chores on their pioneer homestead. Instead, Edden was allowed free time to play the gourd fiddle that his father had made him. As an adult, Edden's adversion to work was legendary.

When he got married in 1892, his new wife tried to lay down the law and told him to go out and get a job to support the family. When he flatly refused, the marriage was over. It lasted about ten days. Edden's second wife was somehow happy to put up with their nomadic lifestyle. About twice a year, Edden, his wife, and their seven children would pack up and move on to a new abandoned farmhouse to squat in. He earned money by winning an occasional fiddle contest, moonshining, hunting, fishing, and whittling axe handles.

It was common in those days for fiddlers to use a flour sack instead of a regular fiddle case. Edden, however, did them one better. The flour sack that he used still had flour in it! When he would arrive to play at a dance or a fiddler's convention, he'd have to blow a thick coat of flour off his fiddle. This normally produced howls of laughter, which was soon silenced when Edden expertly drew his bow across the strings. He seldom took less than first at any contest he ever entered. He was once quoted as saying, "Upon my honor, that's just as good as the best cases every made. That flour makes her play good."

Hot Lick #1. In measure 6, instead of playing that first clawhammer, combine a whack-hammer with hammer-on to the 2nd string, 2nd fret.

Hot Lick #2. Instead of playing the first two notes as written in measures 9, 11, and 13 you can play a hammer-on from open to 4th fret on the 3rd string.

Sherman Hammons

Photo by Carl Fleischhauer

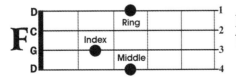

Note. In measures 10 and 14, you'll need to play this F chord before you do your clawhammer.

Greasy Coat

gDGCD - Key of G Modal

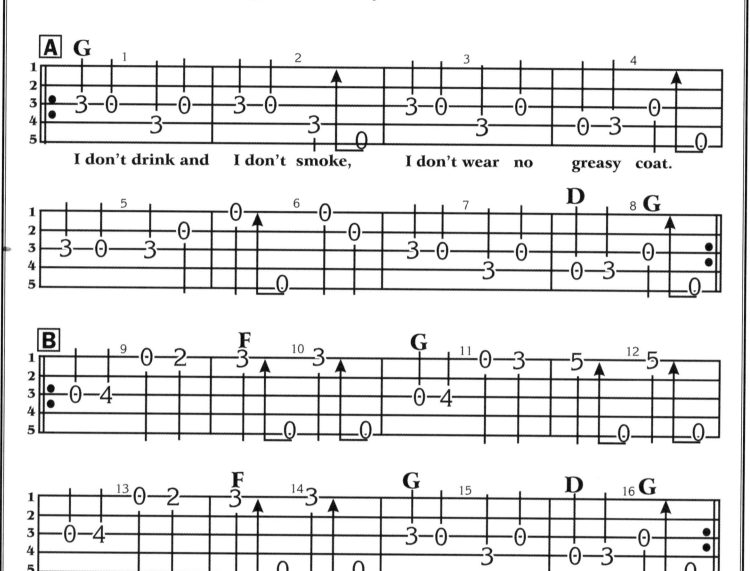

I don't drink and   I don't smoke,   I don't wear   no   greasy   coat.

I don't drink and I don't smoke,
I don't wear no greasy coat.

I don't cuss, I don't chew,
I don't mess with girls that do.

I don't kiss, I don't tell,
And all you sinners gonna go to hell.

Did you hear about the banjo player that was so depressed about
his timing that he threw himself behind a train?

Lonesome John

gDGCD - Key of G Modal

Unlike most of the tunes in this book, "Lonesome John" was apparently not recorded on commercially in the 1920s or 30s. Folklorist Jeff Todd Titon has discovered that John M. Salyer from Salyersville, Kentucky made a home recording of this tune in December of 1941. A number of other Kentucky musicians were also reported to have played this tune, including Glen Fannin, Santford Kelly, Birch Patrick, Peachie Howard, Grover Salyer, Hassell Helton and Leck Risner.

Even though most fiddle tunes have had random or floating lyrics attached to them, so far "Lonesome John" is verseless! Maybe you'll be the first to compose a set of lyrics to go with this tune.

Hot Licks. As you've noticed, most of the tunes in this book are written out with the skeleton of the tune. However, for "Lonesome John," I've written in several hammer-ons and pull-offs to make the tune sound more complete.

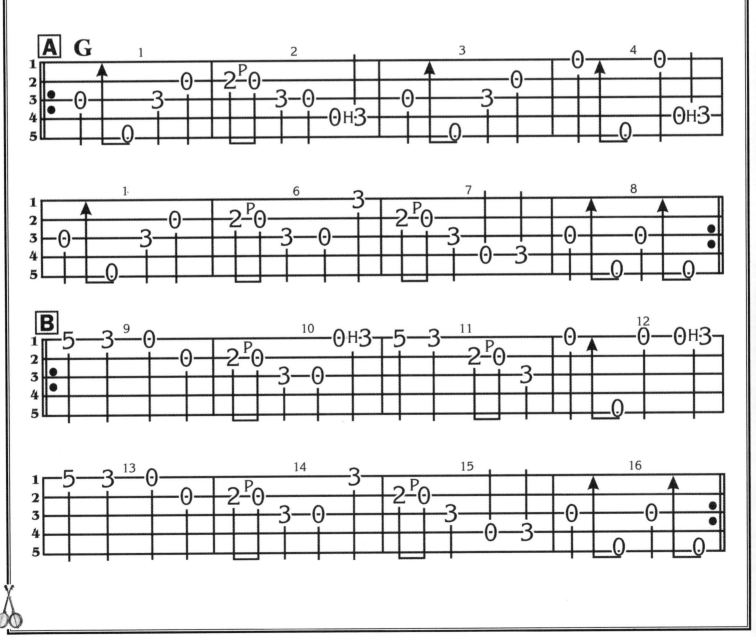

Sandy Boys

53

gDGCD - Key of G Modal

Edden Hammons, from Webster County, West Virginia, was the first known fiddler to play "Sandy Boys." Historian Andrew Kuntz has discovered that some elements of the tune may go back to the minstrel era, and were included in the book, *Phil Rice's Correct Method for the Banjo* (1857). On the other hand, "Sandy Boys" also bears some similarity to the old-time tune "June Apple." In the 1970s, a variation of the tune by fiddler Bob Harring started showing up at Southern fiddler's conventions and festivals. That's the source of this version. Originally, "Sandy Boys" was entirely an instrumental. However, in recent years, a number of "floating verses" have attached themselves to the tune. Some of these have origins in such songs as "Sourwood Mountain, "Shady Grove," "Old Coon Dog," and "Raccoon and Possum, just to name a few.

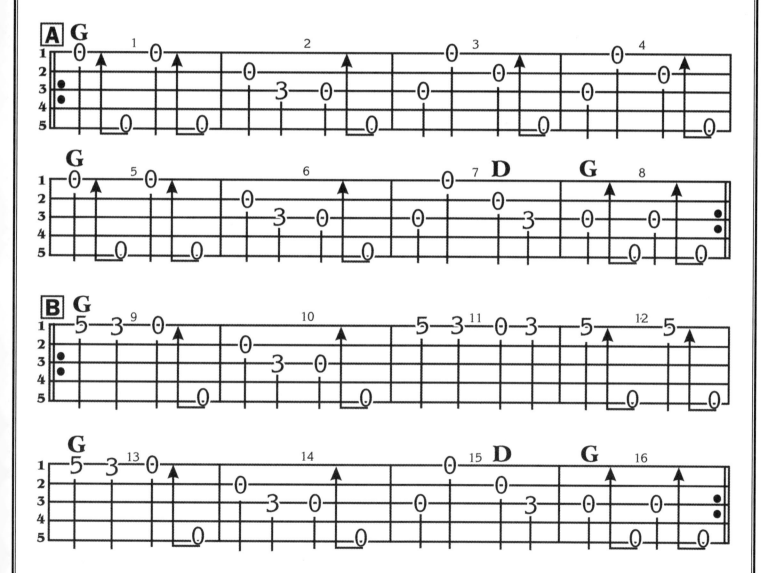

Note: The B part of "Sandy Boys" is very close to the B part of "Lonesome John" on the facing page. Instead of playing the first two notes in measures 10 and 14 of "Sandy Boys," you can play the pull-off in measure 10 of "Lonesome John."

Tater Patch

gDGCD - Key of G Modal

Here's what Tommy Jarrell told me in July of 1980 about the origins of "Tater Patch." "I know the feller that made that tune. He married my wife's uncle. He was in the tater patch hoeing or doin' something and he thought of that tune. It came to his mind. He just quit what he was doing, threw the hoe down, went to the house, got his banjo and played it. Ike Leonard was the man who made it." Like most songs in sawmill tuning, you don't have to be concerned with the chords.

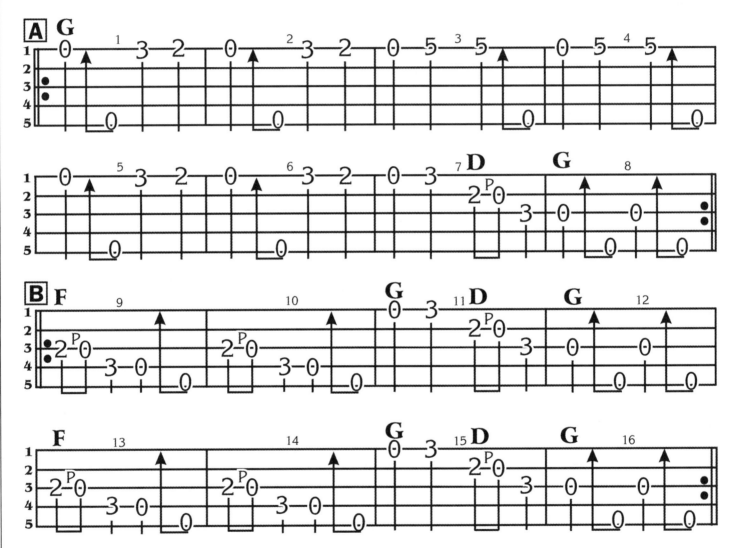

Hot Lick #1. Instead of playing the clawhammer in measures 1, 2, 5 and 6, you can substitute a drop-thumb (page 14). The result will sound like "claw-n-ham-mer."

Hot Lick #2. Add some thumbing to any of the single notes in the first 7 measures of "Tater Patch."

Hot Lick #3. Any time the melody is on the 3rd string, 3rd fret, you can bend that note (page 14) to get a bluesy effect.

Warfare

gDGCD - Key of G Modal

This old gospel song comes to us from E.C. Ball, the great guitar player and singer who lived in the tiny rural village of Rugby in the southwest corner of Virginia. He was neighbors with Wayne Henderson, the legendary instrument builder. "Warfare" is one of those slow and lonesome banjo tunes that sound good played as a solo without any hot licks. You can ignore the chords.

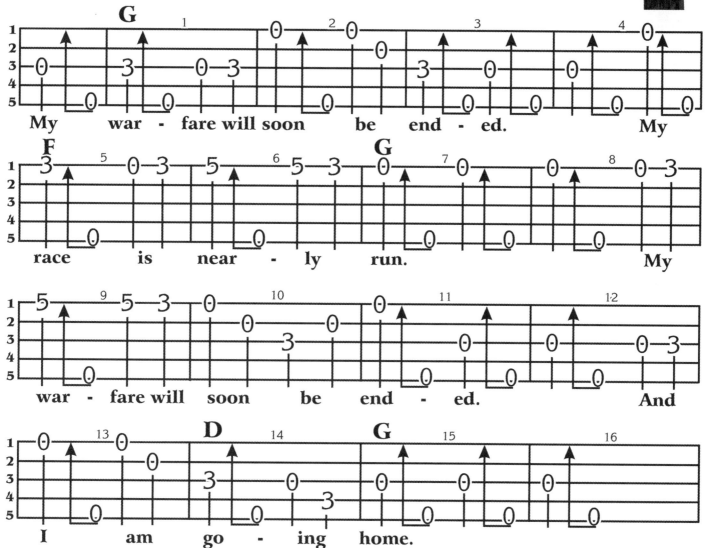

My Lord told his disciples,
After I'm risen and gone,
You will meet with troubles and trials,
But by your rebukes I am strong.

You can rebuke me all you want to,
I'm traveling home to God,
I'm well acquainted with the crossing,
And all my ways are gone.

They say my Lord is a devil,
They call his saints the same,
I'm not expecting any more down here,
Than grief and storm and rain.

God bless them Holiness people,
The Presbyterians too,
The good ole shouting Methodists,
And the praying Baptist too.

Boll Weevil

D7 [chord diagram]

The lowly boll weevil has certainly made a name for himself. Since he crossed the Mexican border into Brownsville, Texas in 1892, things have never been quite the same for Southern cotton farmers. It's no wonder there have been so many songs written about him. As early as March 7, 1924, Gid Tanner recorded the song that would be his first and only solo recording, "Boll Weevil Blues." In that same month in 1924, Fiddlin' John Carson recorded "Dixie Boll Weevil."

This unique version of "Boll Weevil" closely resembles the melody of the black spiritual "Working on a Building." My late friend Ray Alden said that Tommy Jarrell remembered first hearing it sung by an African-American woman who accompanied herself on the tambourine in a traveling tent show that passed through Mount Airy, North Carolina. Tommy liked the song so well that he paid to go back to the show a second time so he could hear the song again. After he had the song in his head, he went home and played it on the fiddle in one of his "graveyard" tunings (DDAD). Some forty years later, while playing at a jam, Tommy suddenly remembered the song, words and all.

We're going to play "Boll "Weevil" in a spooky-sounding tuning that I thought I had made up. I even went so far as to call it "Wayne's D modal tuning." However, I later found out that it was a rare tuning played in Kentucky by Banjo Bill Cornett (1890-1959) who used it on "Buck Creek Girls." In addition to being an ace banjo player, Bill's other major accomplishment included being a Kentucky state legislator. He died while he was playing his banjo, not a bad way to go.

This tuning makes it possible to get that great modal sound of sawmill tuning, except in the key of D. If you're already in sawmill tuning, all you have to do is tune the 5th string down one fret, from G to F#. Fret the 1st string at the 4th fret and tune your 5th string to that.

Your basic chord in this tuning will be a one-finger chord that's actually a D7. **Note:** your guitar player can merely play a D. For most of the song, you can keep your finger on this chord as you play the tune. Ignore the A chord.

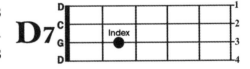

Hot Lick #1. You can replace the 1st note in measures 1, 3, and 5 with a hammer-on to the 2nd string, 2nd fret.

Hot Lick #2. On the first note in measures 7 and 9, you can add a hammer-on to the 3rd string, 2nd fret.

Hot Lick #3. If you'd like to add to the bluesy flavor of "Boll Weevil," you can bend the 4th string, 3rd fret in measures 6, 7, 8, or 9.

A conversation between a newspaper reporter and Tommy Jarrell went like this: "They tell me you're the master of the old time fiddle." Tommy replied, "Now mister, they ain't nobody mastered the fiddle. There's notes in that fiddle ain't nobody found. There's music in that thing that'll be there when Gabriel toots his horn."

Boll Weevil

f#DGCD - Key of D

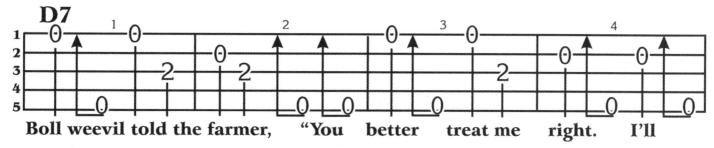

Boll weevil told the farmer,   "You   better   treat me   right.   I'll

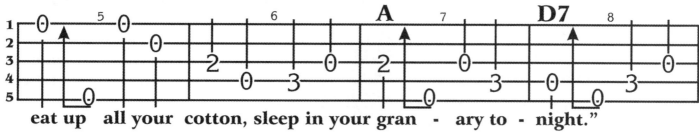

eat up   all your   cotton, sleep in your gran - ary to - night."

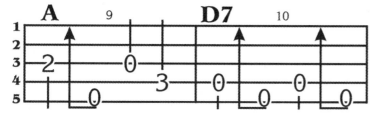

Boll Weevil told the farmer,
"You better treat me right.
I'll eat up all your cotton,
Sleep in your granary tonight."

Boll Weevil told the farmer,
"You'll need no Ford machine,
I'll eat up all your cotton,
Can't buy no gasoline."

Farmer told the boll weevil,
"I can't pay the rent.
You eat up all my cotton
I can't save a cent."

I seen a spider running
Up and down the wall,
He must be going
To get his ashes hauled.

I don't see no water,
But I'm about to drown,
I don't see no fire,
But I'm burning down.

Fred Cockerham & Ray Alden

Log Cabin Blues

By Wayne Erbsen © 2015 Fracas Music (BMI)
f#DGCD - Key of D

In old-time music, there are scores of tunes that call themselves blues. Yet the vast majority of them are not what we would call traditional 12-bar blues. Instead, these are tunes that may just have a bluesy flavor. Some of them were possibly named this way to capitalize on the popularity of the blues among record buyers. Typically, a traditional 12-bar blues has twelve measures (or bars) in each verse. This is in contrast to a "regular" tune that has sixteen bars or measures.

Photo by Wayne Erbsen

To make up for the scarcity of old-time tunes that follow the format of a traditional 12-bar blues, I've composed this tune I call "Log Cabin Blues." I actually wrote it in our 1880s log cabin pictured here. The only time you need to play a chord is when there is a clawhammer lick on the D chord. When that happens, merely fret the 3rd string at the 2nd fret and do the clawhammer. If you're playing with a guitar player, they can play these three chords: D, G, and A or A7. If they want to get fancy, they can play a G7 instead of a straight G.

Note: Be sure to play the D7 chord when you're clawhammering in measures 3, 7 and 11.

Hot Lick #1 Add a hammer-on to the 2nd fret in measures 1, 4, and 9

Hot Lick #2. Blues songs love bends and slides. Any time the melody is on the 4th string, 3rd fret, you can bend those notes. Instead of using a bend, you can slide on 4th string, 3rd fret to the 4th string, 4th fret.

Chords: The only time you need to play a chord is the D7 in measures 3, 7, 11 and 13.

Eighth Notes: Play the first two notes and the last two notes of line 1 as 8th notes. That means they're supposed to be twice as fast as quarter notes. Use one downstroke to get those two notes.

Old-Time Tunes That Call Themselves Blues

East Tennessee Blues, Fiddler's Blues, Florida Blues, Logan County Blues, Carroll County Blues, Huckleberry Blues, Lee Highway Blues, Kansas City Railroad Blues, Left All Alone Again Blues, Poca River Blues, Elk River Blues, Cumberland Blues, Polecat Blues, Tupelo Blues, Natural Bridge Blues, Tipple Blues, Hesitation Blues, Richmond Blues, Milwaukie Blues, Drunken Man Blues, California Blues, Bath House Blues, Coal Mine Blues, Dry Town Blues, Home Town Blues, Leake County Blues, Leaving Here Blues.

Log Cabin Blues

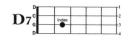

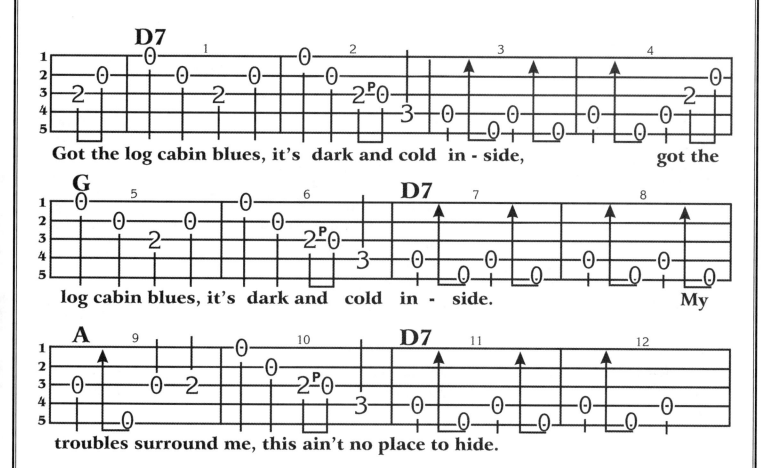

Got the log cabin blues, it's dark and cold in - side,   got the

log cabin blues, it's dark and   cold   in - side.   My

troubles surround me, this ain't no place to hide.

Got the log cabin blues, it's cold and dark inside,
Got the log cabin blues, it's cold and dark inside,
My troubles surround me, this ain't no place to hide.

Gonna take my axe and chop up all of my blues,
Gonna take my axe and chop up all of my blues,
When I get done, they'll be no blues to lose.

The fire is cold and that lonesome wind does blow,
The fire is cold and that lonesome wind does blow,
I've got these blues and I've got nowhere to go.

These cabin walls can't keep out these old blues,
These cabin walls can't keep out these old blues,
I'd lock the door but you can't fool the blues.

The log cabin blues are about to beat me down,
The log cabin blues are about to beat me down,
These blues may kill me, but I ain't goin' back to town.

The log cabin blues have knocked me off my feet,
The log cabin blues have knocked me off my feet,
I'd rather be here than to be on some city street.

Raleigh and Spencer

Blanton Owen & Tommy Jarrell

Folklorist Cece Conway relates the story that in the 1920s, Tommy Jarrell lived just down the road from an African-American musician named Jim Rawley. As Tommy laid in his bed at night, he could often hear Jim singing this song as he walked past Tommy's house when he was returning home from a late night party. Tommy later learned to fiddle this tune from his brother-in-law Jim Gardner, who apparently learned it on guitar from directly from Jim Rawley himself. The title apparently refers to two towns in Virginia and North Carolina that were named after two families from Wessex, England who settled in the area.

"Raleigh and Spencer" is fine the way it is and doesn't need a whole lot of fancy stuff, but you can add a few hot licks if you have a mind to.

Hot Lick #1: Instead of just playing the first note of the song the way it is, you can also slide into that note. Put your finger on the 3rd string, 1st fret, and simply slide up to the 2nd fret. You can do this every time you have the 3rd string, 2nd fret.

Hot Lick #2: You can hammer-on any of the fretted notes on the 1st or 3rd strings.

Hot Lick #3: Any time the melody is on the 3rd fret of any string, you can bend the notes. This increases the bluesy sound of "Raleigh and Spencer."

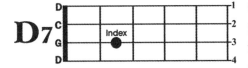

Chords: For the banjo, there's really only one chord in this song, a D7. You need to hold it down while you're playing the tab everywhere except where the 3rd string is played open, as in measures 4, 8 and 10. Guitar players can play D and A.

Raleigh and Spencer

f#DGCD - Key of D

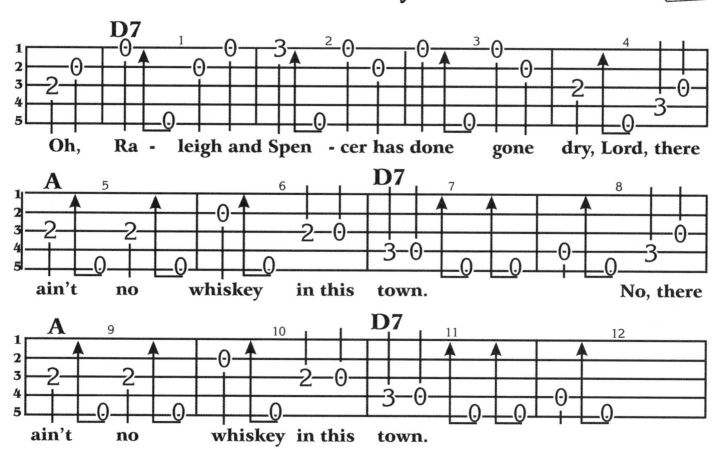

Oh, Raleigh and Spencer has done gone dry, Lord, there ain't no whiskey in this town. No, there ain't no whiskey in this town.

Oh, Raleigh and Spencer has done gone dry,
Lord, there ain't no whiskey in this town.
No, there ain't no whiskey in this town.

I can eat more chicken than a pretty gal can fry,
Lord, I'll tell more of them doggone lies.
Yes, I can tell more of them doggone lies.

You can tramp down the flowers all around my grave,
But they'll rise and bloom again.
Yes, they'll rise and bloom again.

I can eat more fat meat than you can cook in a week,
Lord, I'll tell more doggone lies.
Yes, I'll tell more of them doggone lies.

Q: What's the difference between a good banjo player and Bigfoot?
A: *There have been sightings of Bigfoot.*

Danville Girl

In the late 19th century, there were three hobo or railroad songs that were all kissing cousins: "Waiting For a Train," "The Wild and Reckless Hobo" and "Danville Girl." These songs often shared a common theme of a hungry hobo who meets a pretty girl, asks her for something to eat and then comments on her hairdo, which is "on the back of her head." That was his first mistake. She apparently is from a higher social rank than he is, so she rejects this poor hobo. To console himself, he lights up a cheap cigar that he probably found in a gutter somewhere and waits for the next train to get the heck out of Danville, or wherever he is.

Dock Boggs

The earliest recording of "The Wild and Reckless Hobo" was on February 24, 1924 by George Reneau, "The Blind Musician of the Smoky Mountains." Next to record it was Riley Puckett (6/16/1925) and then Vernon Dalhart (6/1925). These early versions were all set to a bouncy waltz rhythm. Dock Boggs, who apparently came from the "lonesome side of the tracks," recorded what he called "Danville Girl" on March 10, 1927 using a completely different melody. The tune Dock used was in regular 2/4 or 4/4 time, and seems closely related to "Darling Cory" or "Wild Bill Jones."

I learned this version of "Danville Girl" when I had the privilege of jamming with Lee Sexton, the great eastern Kentucky banjo player whose version is close to that of Dock Boggs. Boggs used f#DGAD tuning, but Lee plays it in gDGAD. Not to be ornery, but I much prefer fDGCD, which is an F tuning. It's like sawmill tuning (page 110) except that you tune the 5th string down to F. Merely fret the 1st string at the 3rd fret and match the 5th string to that.

Chords. You can ignore the chords. When your guitar player gets fidgety and wants to play along, they can follow the chords in the tab.

Hot Lick #1. To add a nice bluesy touch, you can bend the 4th string, 3rd fret any time you want. When you use this technique, simply fret the 4th string at the 3rd fret and pull it downward toward the floor.

Hot Lick #2. In measures 4, 5, 13, 14 or when there is 3rd string, 2nd fret, you can add a hammer-on. Merely play the 3rd string open, then hammer on the 3rd string, 2nd fret.

Hot Lick #3. You can add a pull-off in measures 7 and 16 when the melody is the 3rd string, 2nd fret.

Two skunks are walking down the road. One is carrying a banjo. His friend looks over at him and asks, "Why are you carrying that banjo?" He replies, *"Self-defense."*

Danville Girl

fDGCD - Key of F

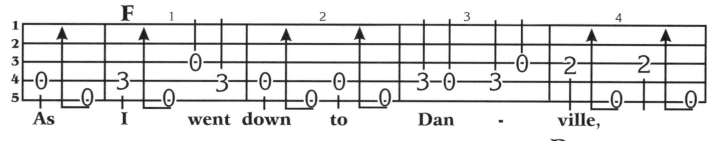

As I went down to Dan - ville,

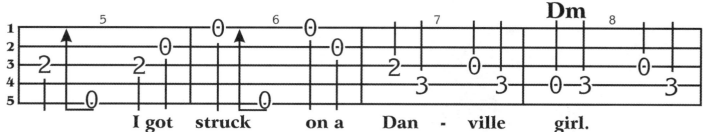

I got struck on a Dan - ville girl.

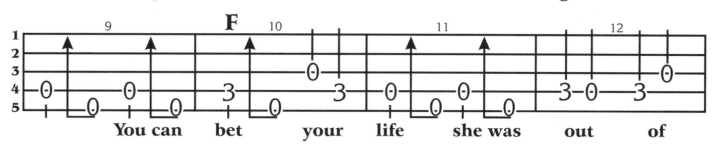

You can bet your life she was out of

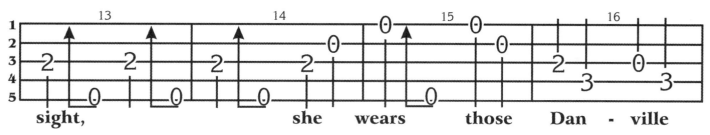

sight, she wears those Dan - ville

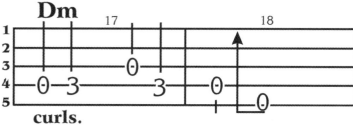

curls.

She wore her hair on the back of her head,
Like most high toned people do.
And the very first train that leaves this town,
Gonna bid that girl adieu.

Standing by a railroad track,
Resting my poor tired feet.
Nine hundred miles away from home,
And not a bite to eat.

I don't see why I love that girl,
'Cause she never cared for me.
But my mind be on that girl
No matter where she may be.

Standing on the old platform,
Smoking a cheap cigar.
Waiting for a local,
Gonna catch an empty car.

Leather Britches

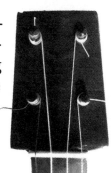

We can trace "Leather Britches" back to the Scottish tune, "Lord Mc-Donald's Reel." Since the time of the Civil War, this tune has consistently ranked right up there with the most popular tunes among American fiddlers. If you thought for a moment that its popularity was because of its ease of playing, you'd be wrong. It's a tough tune to play on any instrument. As my old friend Jack Link used to say, "If you can play 'Leather Britches,' you can play anything."

Even though "Leather Britches" is in G, I much prefer playing it out of F tuning with the capo up two frets. Why? To me, this way of playing it is much more interesting and unique sounding. Keep in mind, however, that this is probably the most difficult tune in this book, so save it for last.

Hot Lick #1. After any of the melody notes that are on the 1st string, you can add some thumbing. This means you can play the 5th string quickly after any of those notes.

Hot Lick #2. As you can see, measure 4 has a lot of stuff going on. First, you'll play the 1st string open, then hammer on the 3rd fret. Then you'll play the 2nd string with your thumb. As if that's not enough, you'll do a pull-off on the 3rd string. After that, you can rest!

Fingering. In measures 1, 2, 3, 5, 6, and 7, use your ring finger on the 1st string, 7th fret and your index finger on the 1st string, 5th fret. In measure 10, you have a lot of real estate to cover. Use your index finger on the 1st string, 3rd fret, your pinky on the 1st string, 7th fret, and your middle finger on the 1st string. 5th fret.

Hot Lick #3. Measure 12 certainly takes the cake, as far as being the most challenging to play. It starts out with playing the 2nd string open, and then a normal hammer-on to the 2nd string, 2nd fret. Then you'll play the 2nd string open, but hammer on to the 3rd string 2nd fret. After that, you'll play the 3rd string open, but hammer on the 4th string, 3rd fret. This kind of a hammer-on is whacky because you don't hit the note you're hammering on to. The secret is coming down hard and fast on the note you're hammering. Good luck!

Chords: By all means, completely ignore the chords. Everybody plays "Leather Britches" in the key of G, so you'll need to capo up to the 2nd fret. For guitar players: F=G, Bb=C, and C=D.

88

Capo 2 to
play in G

Leather Britches

62

fDGCD - Key of F

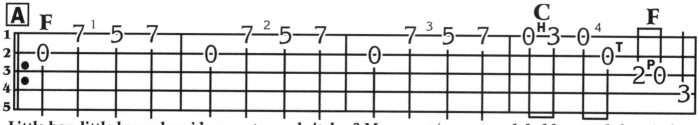

Little boy, little boy, where'd you get your britches? Mama cut 'em out and daddy sewed the stitches.

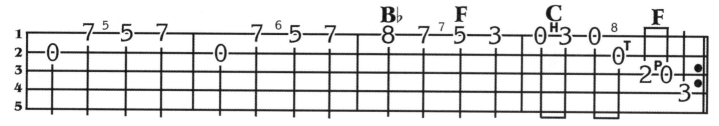

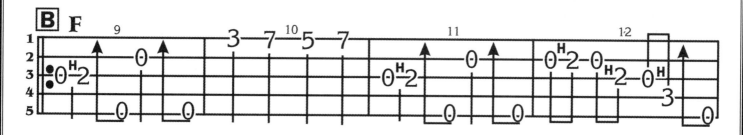

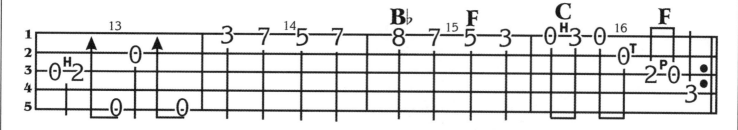

I went down town
And I wore my leather britches.
I couldn't see the people
For looking at the peaches.

I went down town
And I got a pound of butter.
I came home drunk
And I threwed it in the gutter.

Leather britches, finger stitches,
Mammy sewed the stitches in.
Pappy kicked me out of bed
I had my leather britches on.

Leather britches, full of stitches
Old shoes and stockings on.
My wife she kicked me out of bed
Because I had my britches on.

Shady Grove

No banjo book worth its salt should be without at least one version of "Shady Grove." I'm here to tell you that this crooked version is a doozy. It is based on the way I recently heard Lee Sexton play it. If you're not yet familiar with Lee, I invite you to get on the boat. Born and raised in Letcher County, Kentucky, in my opinion he's the most authentic banjo player living on earth. As one of my students recently said, "You can hear the mountains in his banjo playing." For years, he was a drop-thumb clawhammer man, but several years ago he was forced to change his style. As he likes to tell it, he was out in the garden one day and discovered that a coon had gotten caught in one of the traps that he'd set in his garden. In trying to get the coon out of the trap, the animal's teeth latched on to Lee's right hand, and wouldn't let go. When he finally managed to kill the coon, only then did the animal relax its jaws. By then, its razor sharp teeth had already done its damage to Lee's right hand. No longer able to play in the clawhammer style, Lee quickly adapted to a two-finger style similar to the playing of his cousin, Morgan Sexton.

I didn't call this version of "Shady Grove" a "doozy" for nuthin'. First off, it's in what Lee refers to as a "cross-key tune." For us, that means it's an open F tuning. But what really takes the cake is that it's actually in the key of Bb. Don't get your drawers in a twist! This will be easy as eating pie. Oh, and did I mention that the B part is crooked as a rabbit's left hind leg?

Chords. Please don't panic when you see the chords to "Shady Grove." You actually don't have to play any chords at all! However, your guitar player will pitch a fit when he or she sees them. To make it easier on them, tell them to capo on the 3rd fret and play G and Em chords.

Photo by Wayne Erbsen

Lee Sexton

Hot Lick #1. Hammer-ons are a good thing to play in "Shady Grove" on any note that is fretted at the 3rd fret.

Hot Lick #2. In measure 4, instead of playing the 1st string open, you can play the 2nd string, 2nd fret (which is the same note). Then you can play a hammer-on. Simply hit the 2nd string open, and then hammer down on the 2nd fret.

Hot Lick #3. When the melody is on the 1st string in measures 9, 11 and 13, you can add some thumbing. This means you can quickly play the 5th string after any of those notes on the 1st string.

Shady Grove

fDGCD - Key of Bb

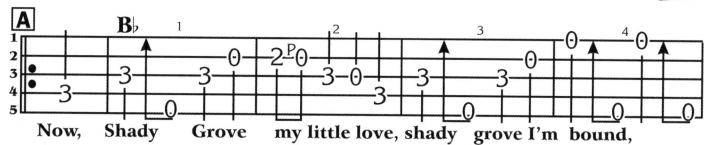

Now,   Shady   Grove   my little love, shady   grove I'm   bound,

Shady   Grove   my little love, I'm bound for   higher   ground.

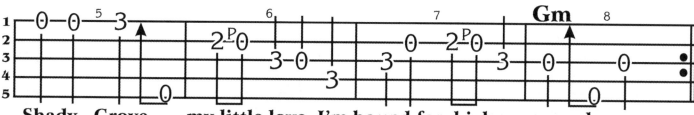

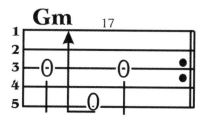

I went to see my Shady Grove,
Standing in the door.
Shoes and stockings in her hands,
Little bare feet on the floor.

Wished I had a big fat horse,
Corn to feed him on.
Shady Grove to stay at home,
Feed him while I'm gone.

Peaches in the summertime,
Apples in the fall.
If I can't get the girl I love,
I won't have none at all.

Lips as red as a blooming rose,
Eyes the deepest brown.
You are the darling of my heart,
Stay 'til the sun goes down.

Blackest Crow

Waltz Time - gCGCD - Key of C

English folk song scholar Cecil Sharp was the first to collect this old ballad under the title "My Dearest Dear" from Mrs. Mary Sands of Allanstand, North Carolina on August 5, 1916. It is also known as "The Lover's Lament" and "The Time Draws Near." This version comes from Tommy Jarrell, who called it "Blackest Crow." We'll play it in double C tuning in the key of C.

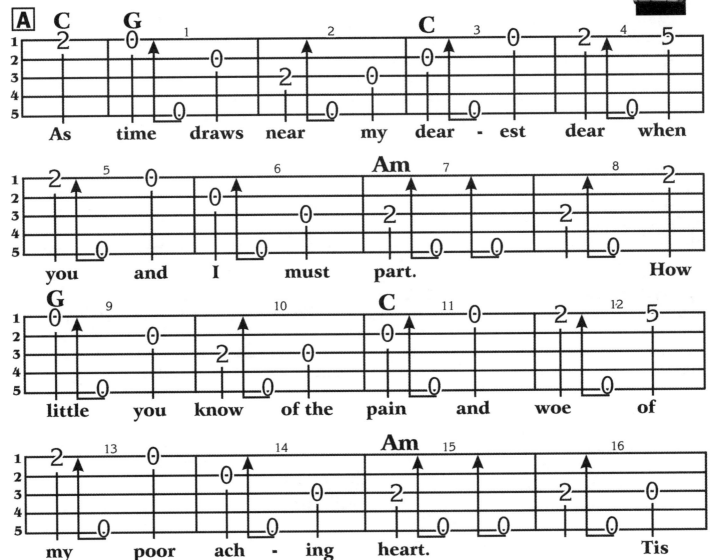

I wish my breast was made of glass,
Wherein you might behold.
Upon my heart your name lies wrote
In letters made of gold.

In letters made of gold my love,
Believe me when I say,
You are the one I will adore
Until my dying day.

The blackest crow that ever flew,
Would surely turn to white.
If ever I proved false to you
Bright day will turn to night.

Bright day will turn to night my love,
The elements will mourn.
If ever I prove false to you
The seas will rage and burn.

Blackest Crow

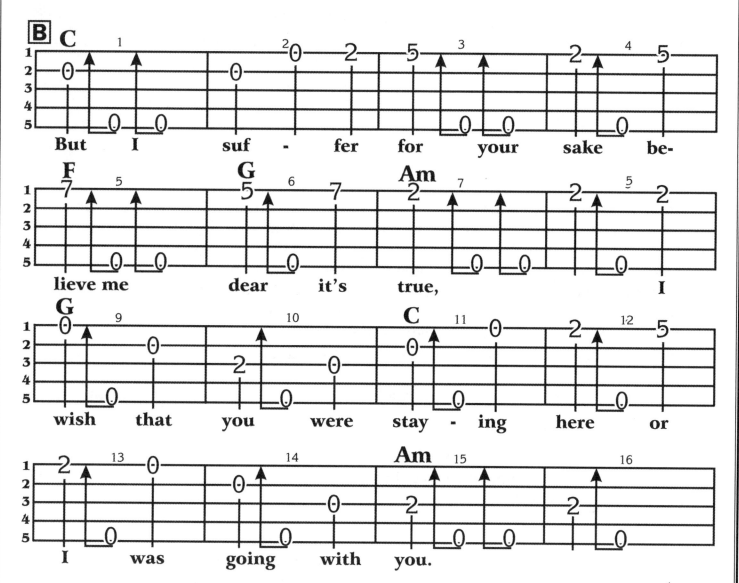

"Blackest Crow" will be our first tune in waltz or 3/4 time. The basic rhythm will be ONE, two, three, ONE two, three. The only thing you need to do to change your regular clawhammer into waltz rhythm is make it sound like "clawhammer-hammer."

Hot Lick: Any time the melody is on the 1st string, 2nd fret, add a hammer-on.

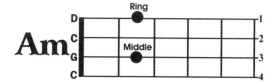

Chords: In "Blackest Crow" you'll need an Am, pictured here. In the 2nd line of the B part, there's an F chord. You can ignore the F and just play the 1st string, 7th fret.

Q: What are the 8 least heard words in the English language?
A: *Let's ask the banjo player what she thinks.*

Gum Tree Canoe

I've always had a soft spot for waltzes on the banjo, and "Gum Tree Canoe" has long been one of my favorites. It was composed in 1847 by the songwriting team of Silas Sexton Steele (lyrics) and Anthony F. Winnemore (melody). During the heyday of the minstrel era it was a popular tune, and the melody was later used for the Civil War song, "On the Fields of Manassas." "Gum Tree Canoe" often goes by the name "Tombigbee Waltz" or "Tom Big Bee River." Among the musicians who have recorded "Gum Tree Canoe" is John Hartford. However, the melody he sang is not the same as the one we're going to play.

Before we learn to pick it, I must tell you a personal story regarding this tune. In the summer of 2014 at the Appalachian Stringband Festival in Clifftop, West Virginia, my friend Ann Porcella and I were singing "Gum Tree Canoe." As we were just finishing it, a stranger walked up and we could see that his face was red, and it appeared that he'd been crying. He said he heard us singing from across the campground and followed the sound to where we were playing. He said that his mother had recently passed away and just before she died, she sang this song. He had never heard it before or since, and he didn't even know the name of it. It was quite a touching moment for all of us and it just reminds us how important music can be.

Chords: The only time you'll need to play a C chord is in measures 4, 12, 16, and 24. In measure 18, you can ignore the F chord and just play the 1st string, 7th fret.

Hot Lick #1. You can add some thumbing any time there are two or three melody notes in a row without a clawhammer. Of course, thumbing just means playing the 5th string quickly after any of the melody notes.

Hot Lick #2. There are numerous places in the melody that need to be gently accented. One way to accent a note is to strum down on all the strings while holding a chord. Try it when the melody is on the 1st string, 2nd fret in measures 1, 5, 9, 13 and 21.

All the day in the field the soft cotton I hoe,
I think of my Julia and sing as I go,
Oh I catch her a bird with a wing of true blue,
And at night sail her 'round in my gum tree canoe. (Chorus)

With my hands on the banjo and toe on the oar,
I sing to the sound of the river's soft roar;
While the stars they look down at my Julia so true,
And dance in her eye in my gum tree canoe. (Chorus)

One night the stream bore us so far away,
That we couldn't come back, so we thought we'd just stay;
Oh we spied a tall ship with a flag of true blue,
And it took us in tow with my gum tree canoe. (Chorus)

Gum Tree Canoe

Waltz Time - gCGCD - Key of C

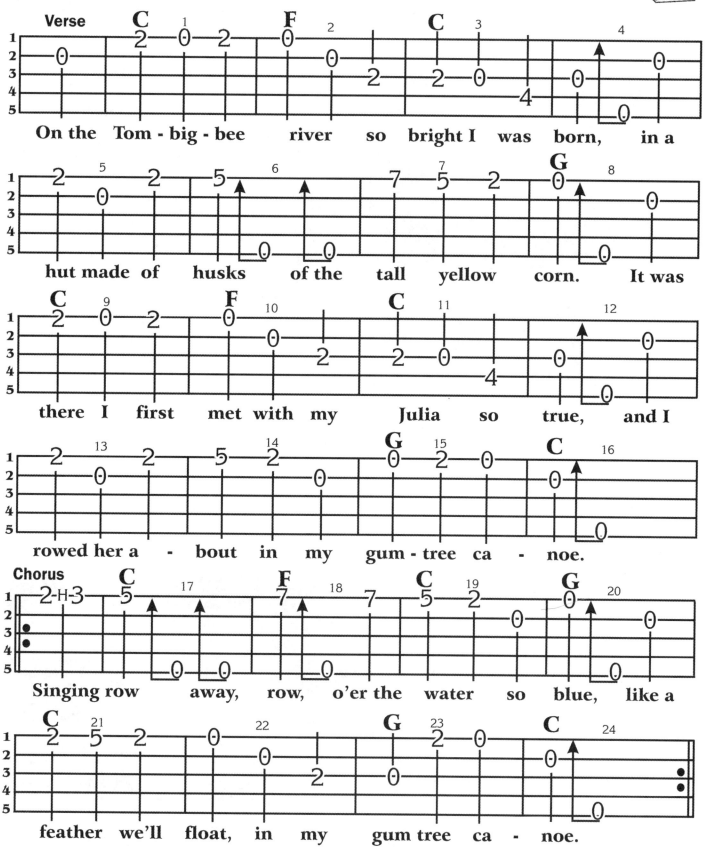

How can you get a banjo player to play faster? *Just wait.*

Knock Knock

Lily May Ledford

Hello in there. Can you hear me through this closet door? **OK, I'LL SPEAK A LITTLE LOUDER.** It must be nice and cozy playing your banjo in the closet by yourself. I'm sure the coats and umbrellas love your music, but we need to have a little chat. It's time you come out of the closet and start to think about playing with other people. The truth is that there are thousands of folks just like you who are also playing in their own closets right now. Some of them play guitar, mandolin, fiddle, dulcimer or just like to sing. Like you, they're itching to get out of the closet and actually play with other folks. Besides teaching you to play banjo in the clawhammer style, I'd be proud to share with you some skills you'll need to jam with other folks. Trust me. As much fun as you're already having with the banjo, it will be even more fun playing with other musicians.

Solo Playing vs. Group Jamming

Of course, it's great that you've learned a number of the tunes out of this book. But it's a whole different kettle of fish to be a contributing member of an old-time jam. There are different but overlapping skills that are needed to be a solo clawhammer player from those of a team player. To be good at playing by yourself, you need to have a firm grip on the fundamentals of clawhammer style, and be able to play convincing arrangements of the tunes. To be a good old-time jammer you need to develop your listening skills so you can follow the fiddle player down whatever path he or she leads you. As my friend Steve Arkin has said, "A good old-time banjo jammer is an interactive player capable of locking in with the fiddler." Experience (and this book) will help you gradually increase your jamming skills. It may not happen all at once.

In the meantime, on the following pages you'll find the vital information that will put you on the path to be an ace old-time jammer. Onward we go.

Doc Watson 1965

There's really only one banjo joke. The rest are true.

Jamology 101

The Jam Leader. At most old-time jams, the fiddle player leads the parade. In a perfect jam, the fiddle would call out the name of the next tune. But, it doesn't always work that way. He or she might just launch into the next tune without warning and the devil take the hindmost. If there's a tune you particularly like, you can always ask, "What was the name of that last tune?"

What is a Key? You've probably eavesdropped on the conversations of old-time musicians at jams and have heard them say stuff like, "Let's get in G." What in the heck are they talking about? By saying "G," they mean the key of G. Knowing the key is important because it gives you at least two pieces of vital information: 1) the set of chords you'll likely need to play the tune and 2) what scale will be used to play the melody. For example, if a song is in the key of G, the three chords you'll usually need are G, C and D or D7. In the key of G, the melody will be based on a G scale (page 110).

Once you know the key, you'll then have to figure out what banjo tuning to use. This little chart will help:

Key of G: G tuning (gDGBD) or F tuning (fDGCD) capoed on the 2nd fret.
Key of A: G tuning capoed on the 2nd fret.
Key of C: Double C tuning (gCGCD) or G tuning.
Key of D: Double C tuning capoed on the 2nd fret or G tuning with the 5th string tuned to F# or A.

What Key Are They Playing In? In most old-time jams, it's common to get in one key and stay there. To me, this is highly annoying, because the tunes all start to sound the same after a while. But hey! Who am I to complain? For you, it's probably a good thing because once you get in the right key, you won't have to worry about changing keys anytime soon. If you're still unsure of the key, it's perfectly OK to utter these words: "What key is this in?" What you don't want to do is ask that question before every tune. In most old-time jams, you can safely assume that the next tune will be in the same key as the last one.

Jamology 101

Courtesy of Jim Costa

More About Keys. Most fiddle tunes are tradition-ally played in certain keys. The most common keys are G, A, D and C. Now and then you'll run across a tune that is commonly played in several different keys. For example, "Golden Slippers" is sometimes played in D, A or G. After you gain some experience, you'll start to remember what tunes are played in what keys.

What Key to Sing In. While most tunes are set in one key or another, singers should sing old-time songs in the key that best suits their voice.

Singing Keys for Men and for Women. Most men with mid-range speaking voices often sing the average old-time song in the key of G or A. If they have a high speaking voice, their preferred key might be B or C. If they have a low speak-ing voice, they might sing in D or E. The only hitch is that you probably won't find an old-time fiddler willing to play in B, E or F, which are considered bluegrass keys. In that case, you might have to adjust the key you sing in, depending on the flexibility and skill of the fiddlers in your jam.

Women usually sing about a fourth higher than men. Think of the Nashville Numbering System, which is explained on page 100. If a male singer is a I, a female might be a IV. To the right is a handy chart that will help you make good guess-es when trying to figure out what key to sing a song in. The top line has the keys for a male with a medium range voice and below are the relative keys for women.

G	A	C	D	E	F
C	D	F	G	A	B♭

Tunes vs. Songs. In old-time music there are tunes and there are songs. Tunes come in all flavors, but they generally share certain things. First, the majority of old-time tunes have two parts, and each part is repeated before going on to the next part. Occasionally, there'll be tunes with three, four or even five parts, but they are not as common as two part tunes.

In old-time music there are also songs. Some songs just have one part, but many of them have two parts, which are called verse and chorus. Sometimes the verse and chorus share the same melody, but many times the chorus has a slightly different melody, with its own set of chords.

Q. What's the first thing every banjo player learns? A. *That Jed's a millionaire.*

Your First Old-Time Jam

By now you've mustered up your courage and you're getting ready to go to your first old-time jam, but you're as nervous as a long-tailed cat at a rocking chair convention. Since you're new to jamming, it might be a good idea to dip your toe in the water before jumping in with both feet. At first, you may want to simply scope out a jam before you join it. Bring along a little pocket notebook or your iPhone, and make notes of what tunes are being played, and in what keys. Invest in a small hand-held recording device, or use your iPhone, so you can nonchalantly record the session. I don't recommend using a video camera as some jammers would be afraid they'll end up on YouTube or Facebook. Make it your business to familiarize yourself with the tunes that are commonly played at a jam you might like to join.

> Old-time tunes are composed of only three ingredients:
> Rhythm, Chords and Melody. That's it!

Rhythm: There are really only two basic rhythms that are used in old-time music. By far the most common rhythm is what we might call "regular time." For those of you who know a little music theory, that's 2/4 or 4/4 time. For the rest of us, that means the rhythm sounds like "one-**two**," or "claw-**ham**mer." The other rhythm that's occasionally used in old-time music is waltz or 3/4 time. That's "**one**-two-three," or "**claw**-hammer, hammer." It's always a good idea in a jam to keep one eye on the lead fiddler's foot. For a tune in "regular time," when the fiddler's foot hits the floor, that's normally the "claw" of your clawhammer lick. When their foot comes up, that's your "hammer." If the fiddler's foot is not in your line of sight, try following the guitarist's foot.

Polk Miller ca. 1900

Playing Air Banjo

Take the fingers of your left hand and lay them firmly across all the strings at the 6th fret or higher. This will mute the strings and produce a chord which I call "nothing." If you do your clawhammer lick on this nothing, or muted chord, you'll get a percussive sound that works nicely for any tune in any key. If you're hopelessly confused about what chords to play, then playing the muted nothing chord is your answer. It actually sounds pretty good and adds a nice percussive touch to a tune. Try it. You'll like it.

Jamming on Chords

What Are Chords? Chords are finger positions that have two or three notes that harmonize with each other. The good news is that most old-time tunes only have three chords at most. Many of them only have two chords.

What Chords to Play? To figure out what two or three chords to play, you need to learn about the **Nashville Numbering System**. This system was invented in the 1950s to make the naming of chords simple. In this wickedly easy system, chords are given numbers instead of letters. The three chords that are commonly used in old-time music are 1, 4, and 5. In this chart, take the key of A, for example, at the top. The 1, 4 and 5 chords are circled so you can see that 1 = A, 4 = D and 5 = E. This system is your magic solution for figuring out what chords go together in what keys.

Key	Ⓘ	II	ⓘⓥ	Ⓥ	VI
A	A	B	D	E	F#m
B	B	C#	E	F#	G#m
C	C	D	F	G	Am
D	D	E	G	A	Bm
E	E	F#	A	B	C#m
F	F	G	B♭	C	Dm
G	G	A	C	D	Em

When to Change Chords? The chords to most old-time songs are somewhat predictable. Virtually every tune will start on the 1 chord. After that, it will either go to a 4 or a 5 chord and then go back to the 1 chord.

Chord Tip #1: The melody of a tune will usually tell you what chord goes with it. That's because the chord normally harmonizes with the melody. If the chord you're on clashes with the melody, then friend, chances are very good that you're on the wrong dang chord!

Chord Tip #2: If you're unsure as to what chord to play, don't make the mistake of jumping around until you find the right chord. A better strategy is to stay put on the 1 chord until it's painfully obvious when to change chords and what chord to go to.

Chord Tip #3: An experienced guitar player in the jam can be your new best friend. To be an expert jammer, you absolutely need to be able to recognize what the common chords on guitar look like. (See facing page for illustrations of many of the common guitar chords). In a jam, I always position myself so I can hear the guitarist, and even more important, see both of his/her hands. Watching their left hand will tell me the chords to the tune or song. Watching their right hand will help me keep up with the rhythm. Memorize the chords on the next page. Once you can "read" the guitarists chords, your job of finding the right chord will be much easier.

Jamming on Chords

George Pegram (banjo) with a fan

The Naked Truth About Playing Chords. In old-time music it's often tricky to tell exactly what chord to play. You have to learn to listen closely to the melody and then quickly decide what chord out of the three would work best. It takes a fair amount of experience to make a good guess about what chord to go to. Many times, the chords are highly ambiguous, and any number of chords could work. When in doubt, ask the fiddler what chords he or she prefers.

Common Guitar Chords

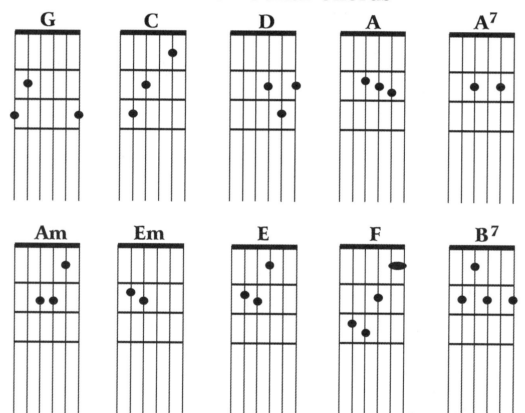

Playing the Guitar

Here's a novel idea. At some point, you should learn to play the guitar. I'm not talking about becoming the next Doc Watson. But, if you are serious about learning to play claw-hammer banjo, being able to at least follow the chords on guitar could be darn useful. It will give you a better understanding of chords, and who knows? When the jam is short on guitar players, you might just be able to step in and be the guitar player. Another benefit of learning the guitar is that you could give instruction to your spouse or a friend who is interested in learning guitar. Before you know it, you'll have a band!

Catching Tunes on the Fly

Playing Strange and Unfamiliar Tunes. Part of the fun of playing old-time banjo in a jam is the challenge of playing tunes you haven't already practiced half to death. At most old-time jams, you'll constantly be confronted with tunes you've never heard before. That's just the nature of the beast. Your goal as an old-time banjo jammer is not to have all the tunes down cold, but to become adept at catching tunes on the fly.

Melody: Not only are there a billions of old-time tunes out there, but there's countless variations on those tunes. Even if you know the tune, it may be totally different from the way the fiddler plays it. Like it or not, it's common practice in old-time music for everyone to follow the fiddler. With a stiff upper lip you must swallow your pride and forsake your cherished version. Your job is to support the tune as played by the fiddler. This is called "seconding" the fiddler.

Grandpa Jones

> **Note:** When you're attempting to jam along on a totally unfamiliar tune, your job is not to get bogged down by all the little notes of the melody, but to zoom in on the important or signature notes of the tune.

The Signature. At the core of every tune is what I like to call the "signature." Some people have called these notes "destination," "anchor" or "landmark notes." Feel free to make up your own name. The signature is simply a short musical phrase that defines the tune and makes it unique. You'll normally hear the signature repeated several times throughout the tune. Once you can learn to recognize the signature of a tune, you merely have to find it on the banjo.

How to Find the Signature: No matter what the tune is, you'll normally find the notes of the signature within the chord that is being played. The good news is that for any major chord, there are only three different notes. That's right, just three. They are called "chord tones." One of those three chord tones will be the melody and the other two will be harmony. If you play any of those chord tones convincingly enough, you'll be in good shape. To understand how to find the chord tones, see page 105.

Trial and Error. The first few times you follow a tune on your banjo, you might guess wrong and land on one of the harmony notes, instead of one of those pesky melody notes. No harm done. In fact, it may sound better that way. A few more times through the tune and you'll get better and better at landing on the right signature note.

The Art of Faking It

The **Same Boat.** Trust me. In most old-time jams you're not going to be the only one who's lost, befuddled, or up the creek without a paddle. In fact, when the fiddler pulls out an obscure tune, everybody's going to be hunting around for the chords and trying to catch that elusive melody as it whizzes by. This is all within the short span of a tune.

Your Memory Bank of Tunes. As you gain experience playing clawhammer banjo, you'll develop not only a repertoire of tunes, but also a store of pieces of tunes. Think of these pieces as interchangeable parts that can be used here, there and everywhere. Keep them in your bag of tricks to pull out during a "banjo emergency."

Artwork by Steve Millard

How to Transpose Tunes From One Key to Another. While tunes are commonly played in one key or another, songs can be in any key. If you've managed to learn to play a song in one key, how do you figure out how to play it in another key? That's the $64,000 question. The answer, my friends, is *not* to look for a tab in the key you want to play a song in. Instead, you should learn the scales for that key. Let me explain.

The Truth About TAB. Before I try to sell you on the idea of learning scales, I've got to tell you the unvarnished truth about learning from tab. Since the dawn of time (actually about 1890), most banjo books have used one form of tab or another. Tab is supposed to be a simplified way to understand the banjo. The truth is that tab doesn't help you understand the banjo one bit. All it does is give you an easy way to know where to find particular notes. That's certainly a big help if you're wanting to play a tune exactly like the tab.

There is one **BIG** problem with tab that you almost never hear. If you're wanting to play notes that are not written down, then you're completely on your own. Tab won't be much help in figuring out where to find those notes.

> "When I'm confronted with a new tune, I just start playing 'Old Joe Clark' and then figure out what is different." David Winston

The Dreaded Banjo Scales

Even saying the words "banjo scales" can send a cold shiver down the spine of even the most grizzled banjo player. Between you and me, that's because even many seasoned banjo players are scaredy-cats when it comes to scales. We might have to bop them on the head to make them realize how valuable scales can be.

Let me tell you what's so helpful about scales. Scales contain all the notes you'll likely need to play a tune. For example, a C tune will mainly use notes that are in a C scale. A C scale is a good one to start with because it's simple. The notes are C, D, E, F, G, A, B. That's it! As you can see, the C scale goes right up the alphabet starting with C. Once you learn these notes, you'll be ready to start picking out tunes without relying on tab. (See pages 109-111 for many of the scales you'll need).

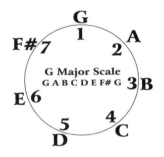

Scales in a Nutshell: A musical scale has seven notes. Let's say we're talking about a G scale. The notes of the scale are G, A, B, C, D, E, F#. If we give them numbers, it would look like G=1, A=2, B=3, C=4, D=5, E=6, F#=7. (See chart on the left).

Let's take the tune, "Row, Row, Row Your Boat." To play the first phrase of the tune in G tuning on the banjo, we would play the 3rd or G string three times. Next you would play the 3rd string at the 2nd fret and then the 2nd string open. The musical notes are G, G, G, A, B. If we give these notes numbers, it would be 1, 1, 1, 2, 3. Right?

Now let's say we want to play the first five notes of "Row, Row, Row Your Boat" in the key of D. First, you would start with your D scale: D, E, F#, G, A, B, C#. Then you would give numbers to that scale. D=1, E=2, F#=3, G=4, A=5, B=6, C#=7. When you get to this point, all you do is play the same numbers we used when we played it in the key of G: 1, 1, 1, 2, 3. Except this time, the numbers refer to the D scale. So in the key of D the first five notes of "Row, Row, Row Your Boat" would be D, D, D, E, F#. Once you get the idea of this, you can simply assign numbers to each scale you want to use. Clear as mud? I hope so.

Teresa Vaughn

A man went to a brain store to get some brain for dinner. He asked the butcher, "How much for fiddle player brain?" "Two dollars an ounce." "What about banjo player brain?" "One hundred dollars an ounce." "Why are the banjo player brains so high?" *"Do you know how many banjo players it takes to get one ounce of brain?"*

The Secret Formula

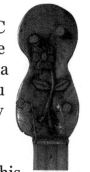

The Secret Formula. Let's say you want to pick out a tune in the key of C without tab. Of course, you would use a C scale. Beyond that, there are three important notes that you'll need: C, E, and G. These three notes are called a "C triad" or a "C chord." To understand how to make your own triad or chord, all you need to know is the secret formula: (1, 3, 5). That means that the 1, 3 and 5 of any scale gives you the major chord that has the same name as the scale.

In the box below are some common scales. Do you need to memorize every bit of this information? Heavens no! But you may need to use the 1, 3 and 5 now and then.

> G Scale: **G=1**, A=2, **B=3**, C=4, **D=5**, E=6, F#=7
> A Scale: **A=1**, B=2, **C#=3**, D=4, **E=5**, F#=6, G#=7
> D Scale: **D=1**, E=2, **F#=3**, G=4, **A=5**, B=6, C#=7
> E Scale: **E=1**, F#=2, **G#=3**, A=4, **B=5**, C#=6, D#=7
> F Scale: **F=1**, G=2, **A=3**, Bb=4, **C=5**, D=6, E=7

What's so special about the Secret Formula: Plenty! With few exceptions, every single tune you can think of will start on one of the three notes of the first chord in the song. Whaaaat? Yes, that's right. I dare you to think of a tune where the first note is NOT in the chord.

So when you want to figure out a tune, merely play that first chord on the banjo and the first note of the melody will be one of the three notes of that chord. In fact, once you learn your banjo chords, you can get away with not even knowing the names of your notes, although it certainly helps. Just to emphasize this point, let's put it in a box, so you don't miss it.

> **Nearly every old-time tune will start on one of the three notes in the first chord of the tune. Period.**

What do you do after you find that first note? Good question! The rest of the notes of the tune will follow whatever scale you're using. The melody will either go up the alphabet, down the alphabet, or stay the same. Keep in mind that many of the important notes of the tune will be one of the three notes of whatever chord you're on.

What happens when the song changes chords? Do I use the secret formula for the new scale? Yes! When the tune changes to a new chord, the first note of the melody will be one of the three notes of that chord too. This gives even more importance to the secret formula (1, 3, 5)!

Improvising with Runs

Walk-ups or walk-downs. Also called runs, these little beauties are good ways to enhance a tune or a song. You have frequently heard them played by guitar, bass, and even piano players. We can't let them have all the fun, so we're going to do some runs too. A run is merely a series of three or four notes that lead you into the tonic or root note of a chord. A run to G will end on a G note. A run to a C will end on a C note, and so on.

Runs in G Tuning.

Here is a 3-note walk-up to a G chord.

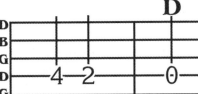

This run walks you up to a C chord.

Finally, this run will walk you down to a D chord.

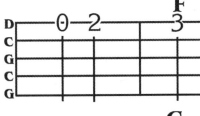

Runs in Double C Tuning.

Here is a walk-up to an F chord.

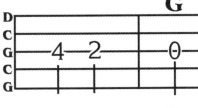

Now try this walk-down to a G chord.

Finally, this is a walk-up to a C chord.

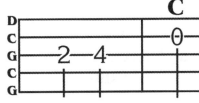

How to put in these runs? As soon as the tune goes to a new chord, time it so the last note of the run happens on the first beat of the new chord. The idea is to anticipate the chord changes, so you're playing the two notes that lead into the chord. Of course, you don't want to over do it, but runs make a good addition to most any tune.

Improvising with Holes

Improvising on a melody is often a dicey proposition. Even for experienced players, it's tricky to make variations on a melody that does not stomp all over the very core of the tune. Sometimes it's a fine line between adding what you think might be tasteful variations on a tune and completely destroying its character.

Here's what I have learned over many years of playing a variety of instruments and trying to improvise in a tasteful way: Old-time music evolved from two distinct musical and cultural traditions: the British Isles and Africa. Each of these approach improvising in a different way. Tunes from the British Isles allow for only a very narrow range of improvising that mainly involve adding ornamentation to existing melodies. These ancient tunes tend to be very busy with detailed and often complex melodies. It's certainly difficult, if not impossible, to conceive of "improving" these kinds of tunes by spontaneously improvising on them.

Call-and-response. Tunes that are influenced by African traditions, on the other hand, are entirely different. On these kinds of tunes, improvising is strongly encouraged and the tunes tend to be relatively simple, which leaves more room for improvising. The main thing to remember is that music from the British Isles basically fills up every conceivable space with notes, while African influenced music leaves lots of "holes," pauses or gaps. That's because African music uses a common technique known as call-and-response. After a call, there's a gap, a space, or a hole. That's where you can add a juicy lick, or some musical figment of your imagination. Let's use "Let Me Fall" (page 62) as an example to illustrate the call-and-response technique.

Samantha Bumgarner

If you're lost in the woods, and you run into a banjo player who's out of tune, a banjo player who's in tune, and Santa Claus, who do you ask for directions? *The first one, because the others are a figment of your imagination.*

Improvising with Holes

Ways to fill in holes. When you are trying to fill a "hole" in a song or tune, the sky's practically the limit as to what you can put in there (within reason). Let's explore a few options, using the call-and-response technique on "Let Me Fall." Keep in mind that the vocalist will be the "call" and the banjo will be the "response."

To the right are the pickup notes and the first two measures of "Let Me Fall." We're thinking of the words "I get drunk" as the "call."

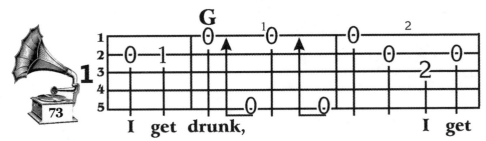

In this example, I have taken out some of the notes and added the notes that go with the words of the response ("I get drunk").

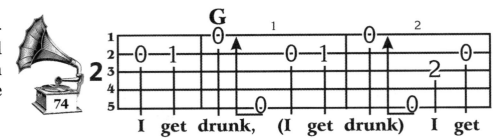

In this example, we can play the "response" backwards.

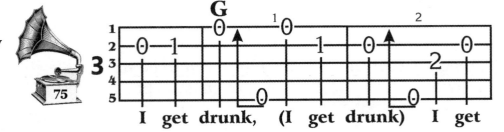

Scales sound so boring but they can be your new best friend. You can use them to fill in the holes. In the case of "Let Me Fall," you can fill in the "I get drunk" hole with a bit of a descending G scale (one that goes down in pitch).

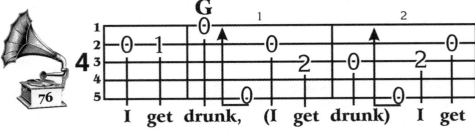

This means you can start on the 2nd string open, then play the 3rd string, 2nd fret, and then the 3rd string open followed by a ham-mer.

As a variation, you can play this same G scale backward, which means you're playing an ascending scale (one that goes up in pitch.)

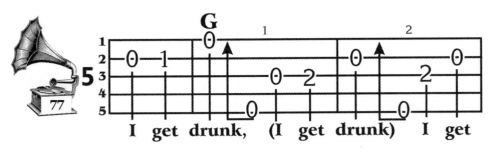

Banjo Tunings & Scales

In this book we use five banjo tunings. Here they are in the order they are presented in the book with instructions on tuning. **Note:** Banjo tunings always start with the 5th string, which is shown as a lower case letter.

gCGCD ~ Double C Tuning

Double C Tuning 1) Tune the 1st sting to a D note from another instrument or to an electronic tuner. 2) Fret the 2nd string at the 2nd fret, and tune the 2nd string so it sounds like the 1st string played open. 3) Fret the 3rd string at the 5th fret and tune the 3rd string so it sounds like the 2nd string played open. 4) Fret the 4th string at the 7th fret and adjust it so it sounds like the 3rd string played open. 5). Fret the 1st string at the 5th fret and compare it to the 5th string played open. Adjust the 5th string so it sounds like the 1st string fretted at the 5th fret. Tunes in double C tuning can be found on pages 16-45.

C Major Scale

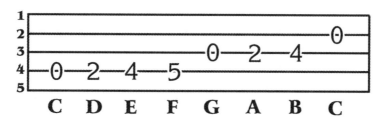

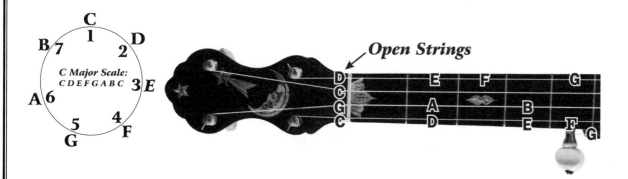

gDGBD ~ G Tuning

G Tuning. 1) Tune the 1st string to a D note from another instrument or to an electronic tuner. 2) Fret the 2nd string at the 3rd fret and adjust it so it sounds like the 1st string played open. 3) Fret the 3rd string at the 4th fret and compare it to the 2nd string open. Change the 3rd string so it sounds like the 2nd string open. 4) Fret the 4th string at the 5th fret and compare it to the 3rd string played open. Change the 4th string so it sounds the same as the 3rd string open. 5) Finally, fret the 1st string at the 5th fret and compare it to the 5th string played open. Adjust the 5th string so it sounds like the 1st string played at the 5th fret. Tunes in G tuning can be found on pages 44-71.

G Major Scale

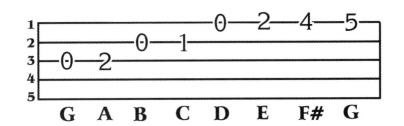

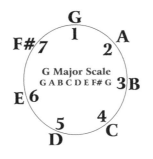

G A B C D E F# G

gDGCD G Modal/Sawmill Tuning

Sawmill Tuning. This is just like G tuning, except that the 2nd string is raised one fret higher, from a B to a C. 1) Tune the 1st string to a D note from another instrument or to an electronic tuner. 2) Fret the 2nd string at the 2nd fret and make that note sound like the 1st string played open. 3) Fret the 3rd string at the 5th fret and play the 2nd string open. Change the 3rd string so it sounds like the 2nd string open. 4) Fret the 4th string at the 5th fret and make it sound like the 3rd string played open. 5) Fret the 1st string at the 5th fret and adjust the 5th string so it sounds like that. Tunes in sawmill tuning can be found on pages 72-79.

G Modal Scale

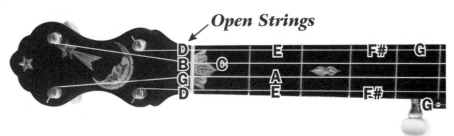

G A B♭ C D F G

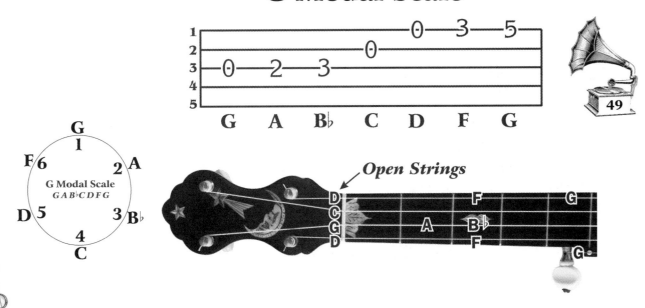

Banjo Tunings & Scales

f#DGCD ~ D Modal Tuning

D Modal Tuning. This is exactly like sawmill tuning, except for the 5th string, which should be lowered (in pitch) from a G to an F#. Fret the 1st string at the 4th fret, and make your 5th string sound like that. Tunes in D modal tuning can be found on pages 76-83.

D Modal Scale

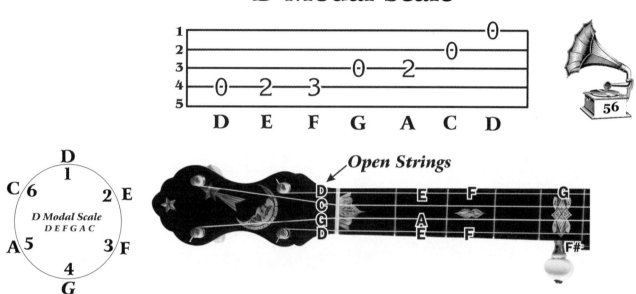

fDGCD ~ F Tuning

F Tuning. This is the same as sawmill tuning, except for the 5th string, which should be lowered from G to F. To tune the 5th string to an F, fret the 1st string at the 3rd fret and tune your 5th string to that. Tunes in F tuning can be found on pages 86-91.

F Major Scale

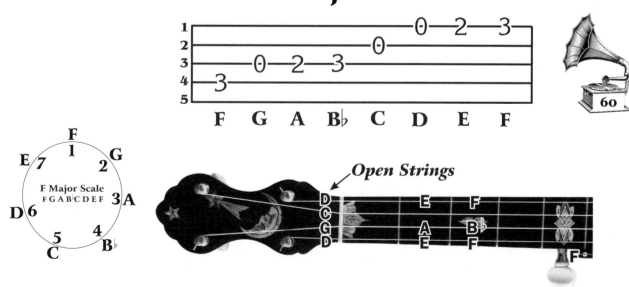

Banjo Chords

Chords in Double C Tuning (gCGCD)

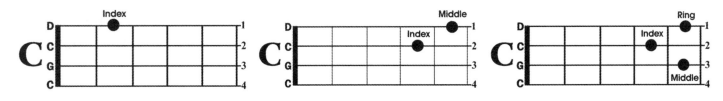

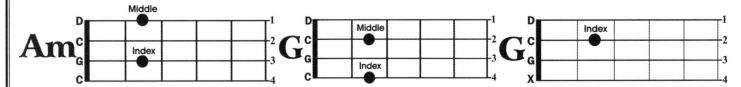

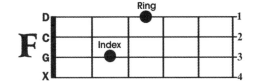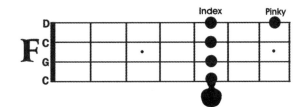

Chords in G Tuning (gDGBD)

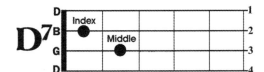

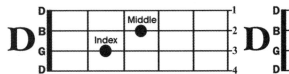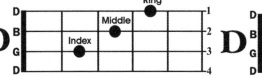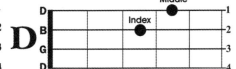

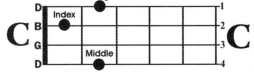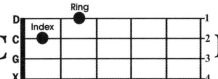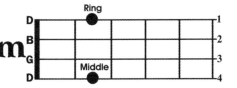

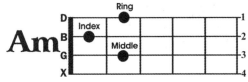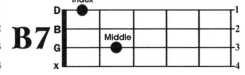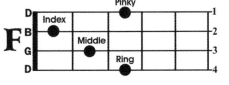

Banjo Chords

Chords in G Modal/Sawmill Tuning (gDGCD)

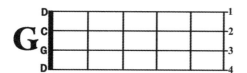

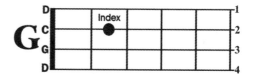

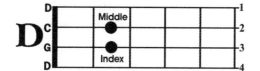

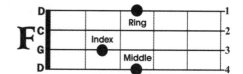

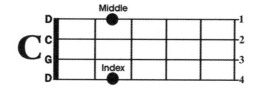

Chords in D Modal Tuning (f#DGCD)

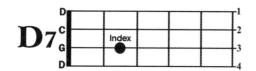

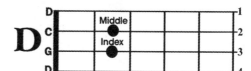

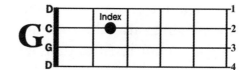

Chords in F Tuning (fDGCD)

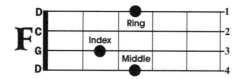

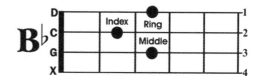

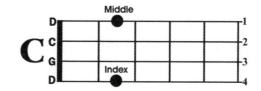

Your Burning Questions

Here are some of the burning questions that my students have asked in workshops and classes. Maybe you've wondered about these very same things.

"How do I know when I'm ready to join an old-time jam?" First, keep in mind that there are jams of all levels, from slow jams to professional. Before jumping into a jam, make sure your level of playing is about equal to that of the other jammers. It's no fun for anybody to have widely divergent skill levels in a jam. As you stand on the sidelines itching to join the jam, remember that playing in any jam requires that you have a fairly tight grip on several vital skills. First, you should be able to change to the right chord at the appropriate time, at least most of the time. Next, and most important, you need to be able to play with good timing. That means you have to constantly be on alert to keep from speeding up or slowing down.

"Should I use a metronome when I practice?" Some people find it very useful to use a metronome to help them keep steady time. In order to jam, you absolutely need to keep a constant tempo. A metronome can help. Remember that the main difference between noise and music is that music must have rhythm. If you're having trouble playing fast enough, a metronome might help grease the wheels. Gradually increase the speed of the metronome until you can make a lightning bolt look like it's backing up.

"How can I get good at jamming if I'm not yet good enough to jam?" Good question! It's definitely a challenge to practice jamming by yourself in the closet, since the very definition of jamming is playing with other people. I think the key is getting certain skills under your belt, such as timing and chords. After that, it's a matter of pulling yourself up by your bootstraps and finding a few sympathetic people to jam with. A good jam partner will accept your foibles if you accept theirs.

"I live so far back in the woods that there's no one to jam with." This is a problem shared by pickers everywhere, even city slickers. It's often hard to find old-time pickers with just the right combination of talent (or lack thereof), compatibility and availability. If you can't find a guitar player, for example, I suggest you learn a few guitar chords (see page 101) and be prepared to train a friend or spouse to play with you. Presto! You're jamming.

"How can I find local jams?" Before the internet, finding a jam often meant visiting the nearest music store and pinning a note to the bulletin board saying that you're looking for a jam. In fact, many music stores commonly host weekly old-time jams. Nowadays, you can use the internet to locate regional or statewide old-time associations which can help you find the open jam nearest you. Other valuable resources include online groups such as Banjo Hangout.

Your Burning Questions

"How can I kick my addiction to reading tab?" After you take the first puff, they say it's really hard to quit. Seriously, people become "paper trained," and it's very difficult to wean yourself off of reading tab. My best advice is to get the melodies of the songs you want to play firmly planted in your head, so you can sing or hum them. Once you have the melody of a song in your head, you'll use scales to help you find those melody notes on your banjo. (See pages 109-111). After you figure out where to find the melody notes of a tune, you just need to add your clawhammer lick. Finally, if you spend more time trying to play by ear than you do reading tab, you'll surely whip your addiction to that wicked stuff.

"What is a 'jambuster,' and how can I keep from being one?" A jambuster is a person or a song that's so inappropriate that it makes people want to pack up their marbles and go home. If you carefully observe an old-time jam before you jump into it, you'll be aware of the kinds of tunes the group is used to playing and you'll be accepted like you were bringing in a homemade apple pie, hot out of the oven!

"How do I keep from deadening the strings with my fat fingers? Your fingers are NOT too fat to fret the strings cleanly! Using proper left hand technique is the key to playing clear, crisp notes. Be sure to use only the tips of your fingers. Bend your wrist slightly so that your fingers are not leaning over and touching the next string. (See photo on page 12). Keeping your nails short also helps.

Is it wrong to use a bluegrass banjo in an old-time jam? Heavens no! If anyone scowls at you for playing a resonator banjo, tell them that many of the greatest old-time banjo players favored banjos with a resonator. If they need further convincing, rattle off such names as Charlie Poole, Obray Ramsey, Bascom Lamar Lunsford, Clyde Davenport, Dock Boggs, Wade Ward and Clarence Ashley. That will fix them.

The main difference between a bluegrass and an open-back banjo is that the bluegrass models have a resonator, and the open-backs do not. The only problem I can see with playing a bluegrass banjo is that the resonators make the banjo louder and heavier. You really don't need either of those qualities, so in the long run, an open-back banjo is probably your best bet. However, I wouldn't necessarily rush out today in your stocking feet to get rid of your bluegrass banjo and replace it with an open-back. Keep in mind that it's pretty easy to remove the resonator, so you may just want to try that option before you spring for a new banjo.

Dock Boggs' Banjo

"I've always wanted to learn to play bluegrass banjo. Should I feel guilty about this and seek therapy? Your urges are entirely natural. In fact, many old-time banjo players harbor the secret desire to sound like Earl Scruggs, but are afraid to admit it. If you've got time to practice both styles, by all means go for it.

Your Burning Questions

"If there's already a banjo in a jam, can I join in too?" That depends. The ideal old-time jam generally consists of one fiddle, one clawhammer banjo, one guitar and one bass. Recently, mandolins, ukuleles and banjo ukes have been welcomed into many old-time jams. If you approach a jam, and there's already one clawhammer banjo player, personally, I would sit out. However, if there are already two or more banjo players, you're probably safe in playing along too. A lot has to do with the attitudes of the advanced players. If they're real sticklers, then I would move on to another session. However, if they seem to have a relaxed attitude, it might be worth asking, "Can you put up with another banjo player in this jam?"

"If someone is singing an old-time song, is it OK to play the melody right along with them while they're singing? Although the practice of playing the melody when someone is singing is strictly forbidden in bluegrass music, it seems to be an approved practice in old-time music. However, when someone is singing, you should lower your volume so the vocal can be heard, and then bring it back up for the instrumental part of the song.

"What clawhammer banjo players should I listen to?" Here's a partial list: Uncle Dave Macon, Stringbean, Lee Sexton, Roscoe Holcomb, Clarence Ashley, Ralph Stanley, Wade Ward, Fred Cockerham, Kyle Creed, Hobart Smith, Tommy Jarrell, Grandpa Jones, Oscar Jenkins, Matokie Slaughter, Gaither Carlton, Sidna Myers, Mike Seeger, Trish Fore, Cathy Fink, Chris Coole, Victor Fertado, Richie Stearns, Seth Swingle, Frank Lee, Jason Romero, Steve Arkin, Emily Spencer, Brad Leftwich, David Holt, John Cohen, Kevin Fore, Tina Steffey, Dirk Powell, Joe Newberry, Bob Flesher, Riley Baugus, Rick Good, Bertram Levy, Adam Hurt, Nancy Sluys, Dan Gellert, Dan Levenson, John Hermann, Mac Benford, Clarke Buehling, Leroy Troy, Mary Z. Cox, David Winston, Paul Brown, Kirk Sutphin, Sheila Kay Adams, Bob Carlin, Ken Perlman, Laura Boosinger, Ben Townsend, Reed Martin, Bruce Molsky, Walt Koken and maybe Wayne Erbsen.

Schlomo Pestcoe Collection

Thanks!

Writing a book is like playing in an old-time band; it can't be done alone. Thanks to Josh Goforth, Annie Erbsen, Barbara Swell and Gianluca De Bacco for editing and Steve Millard for cover design. Thanks to Steve Arkin for banjo advice, Jamie Hooper for photo editing, Tina Liza Jones for illustrations. Front cover photos – from top: Samantha Bumgarner, Sherman Hammons (photo by Marte Clark), Maggie Hammons (photo by Carl Fleischhauer), Tommy Jarrell (photo by Bosco Takaki). Whenever possible, the photos and the tunes are credited. If we have inadvertently used your photo or tune, by all means get in touch so we can give you proper credit in a future edition.

Final Tips & "Free" Advice

Here are various tips, clues, suggestions and free advice to help you cope with playing unfamiliar tunes in a jam. OK, I can already hear you saying, **"What free advice? I paid for this book!"**

Free Advice #1. In a jam, you don't necessarily have to play the melody of a tune. Playing back-up chords is a dandy thing to do.

Free Advice #2. Remember the Hippocratic Oath - do no harm. If you think you might be messing up a tune, relax, lay back and sit this one out. Silence is golden.

Free Advice #3. Even though you may not know the tune, act like you do.

Free Advice #4. Play with confidence even if you don't know what the heck is going on.

Free Advice #5. Be brave when mustering up the courage to join a jam. Assume that you won't know any of the tunes they're going to play, but make up your mind to have a good time anyway.

Free Advice #6. When scoping out a jam, be sure to check the level of players, especially the fiddler. Some players are strict, some are more relaxed.

Free Advice #7. There are many ways to skin this cat. If you don't know the tune, play a few notes of the tune. Or just play the chords. If you don't know the chords, smile.

Free Advice #8. When trying to catch a tune, you may find it useful to try quietly humming or imagining the melody along with the fiddler.

Stringbean

Free Advice #9. My Native Ground Books & Music website (www. nativeground.com) has tons of free stuff that will help you including videos, articles and a blog.

Free Advice #10. Remember the words of Stringbean, the legendary banjo player from the Grand Ole Opry, "There's no money above the 5th fret."

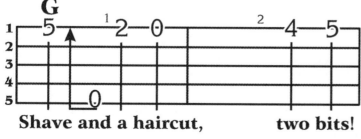

Shave and a haircut,   two bits!

When you're ready to end a tune, you can't beat "shave and a haircut" with a stick! Get in G tuning and leave a poignant pause before the last two notes.

Old-Time Slang

Air - A slow tune meant for listening, not dancing.
Breakdown - A fast fiddle tune designed more for show than for dancing.
Bum ditty - Pete Seeger's term for clawhammer.
Capo - A gadget which clamps on the fingerboard and changes the pitch and key.
Catguts - Strings.
Cheater - Capo.
Clamp - Capo.
Coarse part - Lower part of a tune.
Crooked tune - A tune with extra or missing beats.
Cross-key tuning - Lee Sexton's expression to mean a non-standard tuning.
Cross-eyed tuning - Fiddlin' Arthur Smith's term for cross tuning.
Devil's box - Fiddle.
Devil's riding horse - Fiddle.
Drone string- 5th string on the banjo.
Drunk as a fiddler's clerk - Very drunk.
Fiddlededee - Nonsense.
Fiddler's Grove - Old-Time Fiddlers and Bluegrass Festival in Union Grove, N.C.
Fiddlesticks - Sticks or straws used to play rhythm on the fingerboard of the fiddle.
Fine part - High part of a fiddle tune.
Four potatoes - The four beats at the beginning of a tune that sets the rhythm.
Frolic - An old-time party.
Galax - The fiddler's convention in Galax, Virginia.
Gig - A paying music job.
Hippie Hill - The high ground at the Mount Airy Fiddler's Convention.
Hoedown - An old-time instrumental played at square dance tempo.
Hornpipe - An old English dance tune that was played more slowly than a reel.
Italian tuning - Standard fiddle tuning.
Jam sessioning - Fiddler Ralph Blizzard's term for a jam.
Jig - An Irish tune in 6/8 or 9/8 time or an 19th century minstrel tune in 2/4 time.
Lazy enough to be a good fiddler - A bum.
Lick - A short musical passage.
Mean as a fiddler's bitch - Rather mean.
Mount Airy - Bluegrass and Old-Time Fiddler's Convention in Mount Airy, N.C.
Mountain Modal - Sawmill tuning (gDGCD).
'Ol 5 - 5-string banjo.
Pick up - A truck. Someone you meet in a bar. Notes that lead into the first beat of the tune.
Reel - A lively dance tune in 4/4 time. A dance done in longways formation.
Sawmill tuning - Clarence Ashley's term for gDGCD tuning on the banjo.
Seconding - Playing behind a lead instrument.
Straaaaaaaaangs - Southern pronunciation for strings.
Thick as fiddlers in hell - Plentiful or crowded.
Thumb string - 5th string on a banjo.
To hang up your fiddle - To die or quit.
Turn around - A short musical phrase used as an intro or between a verse and a chorus.
Wires - Strings.

Tune Index

Native Ground Books & Music